The
PERFECT
FLIGHT

Also by Richard L. Collins

Air Crashes
Flight Level Flying
Flying IFR (Third Edition)
Flying Safely
Flying the Weather Map
Instrument Flying Refresher
(with Patrick E. Bradley)
Mastering the Systems
The Perfect Flight
Pilot Upgrade
(with Patrick E. Bradley)
Tips to Fly By
Thunderstorms and Airplanes

The
PERFECT
FLIGHT

Richard L. Collins

An Eleanor Friede Book
THOMASSON-GRANT
Charlottesville, Virginia

Inquiries should be directed to:
Thomasson-Grant, Inc.
One Morton Drive
Charlottesville, Virginia 22903-6806
(804) 977-1780

Printed in the United States

00 99 98 97 96 95 94 5 4 3 2 1

Library of Congress
Cataloging-in-Publication Data

Collins, Richard L., 1933-
    The perfect flight / Richard L. Collins.
        p. cm.
    Originally published : New York : Macmillan,
        c1988.
    Includes index.
    ISBN 1-56566-055-2 (h/c)
    1. Aeronautics. 2. Airplanes--Piloting.
        I. Title.
TL545.C58   1994
629.132'52--dc20   93-48566

*This book is dedicated to the contestants at
National Intercollegiate Flying Association airmeets.
Flying with these sharp young pilots has always
renewed my confidence in the future of aviation.*

Contents

9
Pilots—and the Rest of the World

10
The Future

Preface

FLYING AIRPLANES is one of the most satisfying things that we can do. Maybe one of the reasons for this is that there are so many different things to do, things that not only broaden aeronautical skills but also make for a more complete person. Shoot an approach to minimums after flying a perfect flight. Maneuver an airplane smoothly for landing at a mountain strip. There are a lot of demands in flying; meeting them with skill is a personal achievement.

In flying there are always some trips, moments, events that stand out as special. Many pilots note these in the log, to ruminate over in the future. Indeed, rare is the pilot whose memory is not well entertained by a trip back through the logbook. "October 13, 1981, Beech Field, Wichita, Kansas, to Emporia, Kansas. VOR approach, 400 overcast, mile and a half visibility." That was right after the controllers' strike and one of the first days of the system that required a reservation for IFR flights. No reservation was available.

I was giving Ed Stimpson, president of the General Aviation Manufacturers Association, and his wife Dottie a ride to their home in Washington. We started off VFR, on an ill-advised scud run. When the end of the road was reached, Kansas City Center procured a clearance for an approach to the nearest airport. I finally got a clearance out of Emporia, from the good old boy in the old-fashioned Flight Service Station, but only to a point within Kansas City Center's airspace. Fortunately it

xii was VFR there and we went on to Washington and home VFR. Why is this a pleasant memory? For one thing, I'll always cherish the memory of the Emporia FSS, the last one of its kind that I visited. Clattering teletypes, yellow paper hung on clipboards, and an FSS specialist who treated you like sonny boy. "Sonny boy, if you'll be patient I'll talk them out of an IFR clearance for you." For another, a full Hunter's moon appeared in the windshield when we were flying over Kentucky. Moonrises as seen from airplanes are a treat of nature known only to pilots. There is something wonderful in every flight.

The aviation scene has been an interesting one to me. I soloed in 1951, which was the year of the biggest aviation slump between the Great Depression and the present, and I have worked in the business since. At the airport where I first worked, there was a lot of GI Bill activity; in fact, the bulk of our income from flight training came from that source. Some of those pilots went on to do agricultural work, others flew for FBOs. Few flew for the airlines because in that time the airlines had a great wealth of pilots with heavy transport experience left over from World War II. It was a different environment. The person with Cub and Cessna 170 time from the local airport hardly had a chance.

The first big change was signalled when a doctor showed up in a Tri-Pacer with an "omni" in the panel. He said that this miracle of navigation would revolutionize personal and business flying. We peered at the panel and wondered what was wrong with maps. They cost only a quarter and most of the airplanes were so slow you seldom needed more than one.

The late '50s and early '60s were a time of great strides in airplanes and equipment. Lighter weight ILS/VOR systems became available, and there was a prolif-

eration of light twins and high-performance singles for   xiii
business travel. The range of the airplanes increased
and, given that we had the same powerplants that are
available today, a plateau was reached in the cost-
complexity-payload-performance equation.

But avionics charged ahead and the panels became
ever more capable. The airplanes were improved, too,
with deicing and weather-avoidance gear. By the late
'70s the blush was off the rose and sales of airplanes
started down. Clearly a lot of things hadn't kept pace.
Training standards hadn't been upgraded. The cosmet-
ics of the airplanes failed to keep pace with the inevitable price increases. The price of liability insurance and
litigation increased dramatically in this litigious society. And inflation subsided, which was decidedly bad
for airplanes. We had been paying them off in ever-
cheaper dollars while the paper value remained at
about what the airplane cost. Then it turned around. We
were paying them off in constant dollars, and the paper
value of the airplanes was falling.

The result was a slowing activity, but now it's
about to get going again. One of the favorable factors is
a surge in interest among younger people. The airline
"pilot shortage" is drawing folks to universities, col-
leges, and flight academies in record numbers. In fact,
about half the new licenses issued in the U.S. come from
these full-time schools. The people enrolled in them are
and will continue to be good aviation citizens. While
some in aviation might be gloomy over slow sales or
increasing regulation, these new pilots fly with a fresh
outlook, eager and ready to go. They have to be supple-
mented with a new breed who uses airplanes for personal and business travel, and this, too, will come to
pass.

So ride along from 1951 through the present, with

xiv   a look into the future. The theme of "the perfect flight" represents something that I have always strived for, and I'm sure you have too. Maybe we don't often finish one that is absolutely perfect, but trying to do so every time makes flying a lot more enjoyable was well as safer.

—RICHARD L. COLLINS

The
PERFECT
FLIGHT

1

Liftoff

OCTOBER is one of the best months of the year to fly. The trees below are beautiful and the weather is usually good. If you'll go back through your log, chances are that October is one of the months with the least actual IFR time and the fewest approaches in IFR conditions. It was like that early one morning in late October of 1986. The number on the clock was small— the sun wasn't due to appear for an hour—and the airport was deserted except for the tower. They had just turned the lights on and opened for business.

The mission this day was to go to Washington for a meeting with some industry people on the subject of aviation safety. I had procured the required reservation to land at Washington National and it was the cause of the early start. All that was available was a slot in the 6 A.M. hour. Clearance in hand and cleared to go, I lined up and started forward with the power. The engine came up smoothly and the airplane accelerated smartly. At 70 knots a little tug on the control wheel

1

2   rotated the airplane to 10 degrees nose up and it flew away. Magic, it's always like magic to me. The person with me this morning was not an airplane pilot—hang gliders were his choice—but when I remarked to him that it always seems like magic, he responded, "Yes it does, it really does." I could tell that he was as taken by the moment as I was.

There was some nostalgia to that takeoff because it came almost 35 years to the day after my first takeoff alone. October 25, 1951, Harrell Field, Camden, Arkansas. My flight instructor, Rudy Peace, had worked hard at insuring that I was ready to fly. I lined the Aeronca, N1154E, up on the runway and opened the throttle with some trepidation. There was a little weaving on the takeoff, then the airplane was off the ground. Hot damn, I thought, you have gotten it off the ground, now the challenge is to get it back down safely. Despite the excellence of the instruction that I had received up to that point, it was at liftoff on first solo that I really started learning how to fly.

Thirty-five years later, after liftoff from Trenton on a beautiful morning, I thought that I am still learning about flying. The part about wiggling the pedals and moving the wheel was more or less mastered some years back, but there is so much more to flying than manual skills. And that's the great fun of it: Learning how to do things with an airplane, and to make the airplane deliver the desired service—be it transportation, recreation, agricultural, or some other useful activity. This is being written right after the Voyager's successful around-the-world flight, and that has to be one of the best examples of people continuing to learn how to do bigger and better things with airplanes. Challenges of that magnitude are not available to most of us, but we can and should approach flying with the same

sense of seeking excellence and discovery. Learning   3
how to do it and learning how to do it right are two
entirely different matters. Flying the perfect flight
should always be the goal.

DOING IT RIGHT

Take that flight to Washington. What challenge could
possibly be found on a relatively short flight in a familiar airplane on a morning with good weather? One has
but to think through any flight to find plenty of challenges to skill. But was something new learned? You
bet. Or at least some old lessons were relearned.

Although this was an IFR flight, I learned a strong
lesson in VFR navigation on the approach into Washington. "Follow the Anacostia River inbound for a visual approach to Runway 21." Okay, ace, the challenge
is an early sighting of that river because it is the key to
doing this properly. I go to Washington a lot so the area
is familiar enough to me. Usually the trip down the
Anacostia is at 2,000 feet and you can keep the speed
up until passing Robert F. Kennedy Stadium, on the
north side of the river. Then start slowing down. Entry
is onto sort of a left base for 21, as the river doesn't quite
line up with the runway. All that was in mind, but I still
didn't see the river. It was a hazy morning and what I
learned was to make a note of the radial and distance
from Washington where you pick up the river when
inbound from over Baltimore. That seems a simple
thing, but knowing this can eliminate a perplexing moment, and eliminating those moments when there are
more questions than answers is a good thing to do.

4 ROLLING DOWN THE RUNWAY

A bit later in the day the mission was to fly from Washington National to Vero Beach, Florida. I dutifully listened to the automatic terminal information service and then called and got my clearance. The ground controller then cleared us to Runway 36. It was a warm day, the tanks were full because Vero is a maximum-range trip from Washington in a Cessna 210, and there were three guys and baggage on board. The airplane was a couple of hundred pounds below gross weight but still heavy.

Cleared to go I came up with the power. The airplane seemed sluggish in its acceleration and as I waited for the airspeed to increase to 70 knots, I reminded myself that it was on this very same runway that Air Florida's 737 came a cropper on a takeoff on which the acceleration was slow. But the manifold pressure and rpms were right up there and the runway was long, at least long for a Cessna. Finally 70 knots came and we flew away.

What did I learn from that? To always look at a wind sock before taking off. Because the wind was light I didn't pay a lot of attention to the ATIS—I was going to whatever runway was assigned anyway—and because the wind was light I didn't look for a sock. There was a slight downwind component on the runway, though, and seven or eight knots on the tail on a warm day in a heavy airplane can make quite a difference. My knowing that there was some downwind component would not have made any difference in the airplane's performance, but it would have enabled me to anticipate what was about to happen.

DIFFERENT COCKPIT

The last time I had the engine in my 210 overhauled, I leased a new Mooney 252 to use in my travels and for evaluation. I had flown the airplane before, and flew it from Waco, Texas, to the Mooney plant in Kerrville, Texas, in a form of checkout. I am a firm believer in more of a checkout than that, but because I fly a turbocharged airplane all the time and because I have flown other models of the Mooney frequently, I felt it okay to go on my way solo in good weather without formal ground school and flying in the airplane. It was certainly legal and there was no insurance problem in doing this. And it worked fine.

The airplane was flown day and night, VFR and IFR, without much of a hitch. But once I learned the lesson that all pilots learn when in a cockpit that isn't as familiar as your own living room. The controller had called with word to descend. The airplane was being ably flown by its King autopilot, and while I was setting the new altitude in the window, I reached for the autopilot pitch control switch to get a little descent started. What I learned was not to push any switch without first looking at that switch. The one that attracted my finger was also one that would make the airplane descend—it was the primer switch, located right next to the autopilot, and pressing it causes a momentary power interruption. When you press a switch that does that, you do let go quickly.

THE BIGGEST CHALLENGE

Everyone has a different list of challenges in learning how to fly. The list might well be determined by how much ground school a person had, and by the basic flight instructor's ability to explain things.

6   An early challenge that still stands out in my mind is the crosswind landing. My instructor would patiently explain how it was supposed to work, and I would clumsily try to follow his directions. Time and again he would have to take the controls at the last minute lest we hit going sideways. This was going on in a Cessna 140, which would do a pretty fancy ground loop if you landed with much drift.

My instructor was a proponent of landing with a wing down, into the crosswind. One day he made just the right selection of words in telling me how to land in a crosswind. "Loosen up," he said, "loosen up and use the ailerons to keep the airplane going down the runway and use the rudders to point it straight while you do that." Next time around I used that left aileron to make the airplane track down the center of the runway and right rudder to point the nose straight down the runway. It worked and I never again had trouble knowing what to do in a crosswind. Doing it well every time is another matter.

The runway at this airport was a north-south one and when the wind was strong, it was more often than not out of the northwest, after passage of a cold front. And to this day I prefer managing a left crosswind— probably because in the learning process most of the strong crosswinds with which I had to deal were from the left.

SPEED MANAGEMENT

When I got my multiengine rating, in a Cessna T-50 "Bamboo Bomber," the inspector remarked that I flew the airplane okay but really needed to work on speed control. He said that in shooting three landings I never came across the fence at the same speed twice. To that

point I think I always thought of approach speed as one   7
that you flew at or above. That was not the way to look
at it, and when an airplane is giving trouble on landing
I can usually trace it to poor speed control on final.
There is a correct speed for every approach, and flying
that correct speed is as important as anything that we
do in flying.

I learned a good lesson about this flying the Concorde simulator. Concorde has an autothrottle system:
Set the airspeed in the system and the throttles move
automatically to maintain that speed. You might think
that takes all the work out of it, but no. The pilot's job
becomes that of maintaining the proper pitch attitude,
which is 10.5 degrees nose-up. Not 10 and not 11. The
airplane demands precise speed and attitude control on
final.

I think most pilots have some trouble managing
speed on final. When riding airliners you sometime feel
a lot of power and pitch changes on final. Watching
other pilots fly light airplanes, I see a lot of throttle
jockeying on final. Whenever this happens, and there is
no wind shear, it is apparent that the pilot has gotten
behind on the basics.

I learned a lesson on this in the Mooney 252. My
landings in the airplane were about "half," as we used
to say in Arkansas. That's half bad and half good. I
knew that the Mooney is very sensitive to approach
speed and that too much speed means trouble. Once the
airplane is in the ground cushion, it decelerates very
slowly and, especially when full flaps are used, the airplane has to be well slowed before touchdown lest it
touch on all three wheels, or on the nosewheel first. A
porpoise can result from a level, fast landing.

Seventy-five is the magic number in the Mooney.
Any speed over the fence in excess of 75 knots means

8   a more difficult landing. This airplane had speed brakes on it, okayed for use during landing, and on a landing at Nashville, Tennessee, I tried to fudge and use an 85-knot speed with the brakes out. The landing wasn't good. The worst landing came when some wind shear had been reported, and was there. The approach was correct to begin with, but when the airplane settled into the shear it lost five knots and developed a sinking spell. I gave it too much power and the result was an arrival over the threshold at 85 knots. The airplane touched very softly but flew back off the runway. I landed it a few more times before that approach was concluded. I had finally learned that 75 is plenty even though it seems slow, and that it doesn't take much power to recover from a sinking spell in a Mooney.

ICE LESSON

There are some things in aviation where learning can be fraught with peril. Ice is one of these things. Even pilots who fly a lot do not see a lot of ice, and one of the most important lessons is that ice has to be dealt with quickly. If there is enough ice to accumulate rapidly, there is enough ice to cause a major problem.

I was flying a Twin Comanche that my father and I leased; the trip was from Oklahoma City back to New Jersey one winter day. It was stormy and the elements stood ready to give lessons.

There was a strong low over Arkansas so the best-looking deal was to go north of a straight line between the two points. The flight to Quincy, Illinois, for a fuel stop was without event. But while taxiing in on the freshly snow-covered surfaces, snow was blown back on the brakes, which were hot. The melting snow froze on the brakes while gas was being pumped into the airplane, and when I got ready to go the twin wouldn't budge. A good man at the FBO warmed the brakes with a torch and sent me on the way with the admonition, "Sonny, don't ride the brakes when you are taxiing in snow." As it turned out, if he had really wanted to do me a favor, he would have left the airplane frozen to the ground.

The weather was marginal VFR, and I had let the briefer talk me out of IFR because of a forecast for icing in the clouds. Headed east, following progress on sectional charts, the flying wasn't bad. The ceiling was relatively low, but the visibility beneath was good. Then Mother Nature decided it was my turn. A big raindrop hit the windshield, splattered, and froze. Then another, and in a moment it was raining. The books all say that you can climb to warmer air above, because it has to be warmer above to have freezing rain. But in just a couple of minutes I had an opaque windshield and an airplane that was protesting its load of ice.

I was only about 30 miles from Indianapolis so I called them and explained the predicament. They gave me an immediate IFR clearance and I climbed up into the clouds but it was obvious I wasn't going to climb very high. The only decision that seemed right was a landing at Indianapolis as soon as possible. They gave clearance for an ILS, which I had to have because I couldn't see out ahead and with ice all over the airplane I didn't want to be trying to slip to see. Also, they were now reporting freezing rain at Indy, so any slipping approach would just ice the side windows.

The ILS and the landing worked well enough, but I simply could not see to taxi so they sent out a vehicle with a gumball machine on top to guide me in.

That and similar ice encounters taught me that at the first sign of the stuff, you had best get with the

10 program. And even if prompt action is taken, there might be times when you have to land an airplane with ice on it. This can be the hardest part. In fact, most ice accidents happen as the pilot is maneuvering the airplane for landing. Also, the extension of flaps can do strange things to some airplanes when they have ice on them. Elevator effectiveness might be lost and that is certainly something to avoid.

In that icing encounter, I knew that I was trespassing. The ingredients for ice were there. And while I would probably defend the decision to launch the flight because there no reports of icing, the defense is relatively weak. I knew then and know now that the area north of a strong low is a good place to find ice, and it was certainly there.

THINGS THAT GO BUMP, DAY OR NIGHT

When we first learn to fly, there is some emphasis placed on practicing forced landings. I always had the feeling that the emphasis was in direct proportion to the flight instructor's experience with actual engine failures. An instructor who had left a few airplanes in pastures might be a lot more likely to give forced landings to a student than an instructor who has never had an engine miss a beat. Around the airport where I learned to fly we talked a lot about engine failures, but nobody had ever experienced one for reasons other than having the fuel selector on a dry tank or having air instead of fuel in the tanks. We did forced landings, but the emphasis was not great—and this was in 1951, when engines were far from being as reliable as they are today. The engines that we heard about failing at other airports were surplus World War II engines that had been stored for a long time.

But if there is anything to learn about things break-
ing, it is that most of the moving parts in an airplane will
eventually break, and if you fly long enough you will see
this happen. Some pilots see it early in a flying career;
others see it later. The word "luck" really has no place
in aviation, so let's say the where and when of component failures is a random thing. And that's why we, as
pilots, had best learn early in the game how to handle
the failure of moving parts in airplanes.

It can be argued, with good sense, that the prevention of failures is the first step. The folks who sell bur-
glar protection equipment will tell you to start outside
your house, with light systems. In the airplane, prevent-
ing intrusion by gremlins starts with the logbook and
the shop.

The engine and prop of an airplane have a recom-
mended time between overhaul and few pilots fly in the
face of this number. If you rent airplanes, the FBO can
get a small extension on this time, but that's it. If you
have your own airplane there is no requirement to abide
by the TBO (Time Between Overhaul), but most people
follow the guidelines as far as hours go. What most
don't do is follow the TBO as it relates to calendar time.
All those TBO hour numbers are based on flying a certain amount each month—usually from 30 to 40 hours—
so if it's a 2,000-hour engine based on 40 hours a month,
it is also a 50-month engine. Past abiding by the TBO,
good maintenance is what keeps engine trouble at bay.

There's another key ingredient, one that comes at
the next step—after the engine develops a problem.
That is to not take off unless engine operation is exactly
normal, and to land quickly at the first sign of internal
engine trouble.

I only flew a Stinson Station Wagon once in my life.
The fellow who owned the airplane was a low-time

12   pilot; I was a flight instructor. He said that he was apprehensive about the engine and suggested we go flying and see if he was just spooked. My idea was to leave him behind. I'd just hop the airplane around the patch solo to see if I could hear anything.

The runup was fine, and while the engine didn't sound quite right, I had never flown with a Franklin engine before and didn't really know what one sounded like when it was "right." Line up on the runway. Full power. Feels okay, tail up, lift off. There followed a clamor under the cowling that could only be cause for an abort. I pulled the throttle back and made my first Stinson landing. After a couple of bounces I had the airplane under control and was able to stop it in the confines of the airport. The engine was still running, sort of, but it was shaking. If I recall correctly, we pushed it back to the hangar. It had suffered what might be called a "massive" internal failure.

Not long after that, a J-3 Cub in our U.S. Army–sponsored flying club developed a strange malady. When it was idling on the ground, it whistled. It was also using a lot of oil. We had very limited maintenance capability available to the club at the Army Air Field, so I decided to fly the Cub a few miles to the FBO that did our maintenance. It was not running well toward the last, and for years I kept the piston with the hole burned in it as an ashtray. The whistle was from an intake leak. This caused one cylinder to run exceptionally lean, burning a hole in its piston.

TELL BY THE SMELL

Odors can do you a lot of favors in an airplane. Certainly anything that seems unusual to the nose should be cause for pause. The best story I have heard about

this involves two pilots who stopped for lunch and one
had some beans with lunch. On the subsequent takeoff, concurrent with power application on the airplane, this pilot did what comes naturally after eating beans. The subsequent smell in the airplane was alarming, and the takeoff was aborted for fear something was being incinerated in the engine compartment.

An example of how and why it pays to be suspicious came in my 210 as it aged. For a couple or three flights I thought that I smelled fuel when I opened the door. I asked others to sniff; nobody smelled anything. And the odor went away as soon as the ventilation started through the cabin. But I decided that I didn't care if nobody smelled anything. I thought I had smelled fuel. And when the folks in the shop took out the inspection plates on the floor there was indeed a strong fuel odor. Further investigation revealed that the reservoir tank in the fuselage belly was leaking and needed replacement.

There are times on any flight where the risk increases. Takeoff and initial climb is one of these times unless you fly Transport Category airplanes. And it's a pure fact that if you go on with the departure proceedings without perfect powerplant operation—and that includes no unusual odors or noises—things can get worse before they get better.

TWIN TAKEOFF

He always had a devil-may-care attitude about flying. But he had owned and flown airplanes for a long time so that made it okay. At least it was okay until something happened.

On the fateful flight, he had trouble starting one of the engines of the light twin. Finally, when it did start,

14 witnesses reported that engine operation did not sound normal. Despite this, he taxied out, and, instead of back-taxiing to the end of the runway, he started the takeoff without using a thousand or so feet of a runway that was about 4,000 feet long. The rest of the story is a sad one. The engine that had been hard to start gave up the ghost when the airplane was just off the ground and beginning to climb. The pilot subsequently lost control of the airplane and a disastrous crash followed.

Once you get going, anything the engine does that reflects unusual operation should be analyzed and, if it is suspicious or continues, the airplane needs to be taken to the nearest runway. It can be tempting to continue as planned even though the engine is "a little rough," but there is seldom remission in whatever causes an engine to run rough. Single or twin, the airplane is easier to land before an engine failure than after.

THE SMALLER PARTS

When delving into the troubles we have with airplanes, the smaller parts are more likely to pose mechanical challenge than the larger parts. An engine failure or problem is just as serious when caused by a magneto as when caused by a cylinder. An electrical failure can leave it dark, cold, and quiet; a failure of power to instrumentation or the failure of instruments can leave a pilot at a strong disadvantage. It is in this area that we have learned the most in recent years.

A company that makes air pumps used to power flight instruments in singles and light twins sent out a service letter to owners of airplanes that have, or might have, their pumps. It was like a number of service letters spawned by burgeoning product liability litigation.

The warning was that failure to follow instructions may result in death, injury, or property damage. The instructions were that a backup power source for air-driven gyros, or a backup electric attitude indicator, must be installed in aircraft that are flown IFR. Further, any inoperative component of the gyro system, or any inoperative backup system, should be fixed before the next flight. And finally, this warning must be retained in the pilot's operating handbook.

Whether or not this is mandatory coming from a manufacturer instead of in the form of an FAA airworthiness directive is a moot point. The fact is that air pump life cannot be accurately predicted and the pumps can fail without warning. When they do fail and there's no backup, the pilot is left to fly partial panel, without the gyro instruments that are the cornerstone of instrument flying. History has shown that the average pilot is in trouble on partial panel, especially if flying an airplane with retractable landing gear where the margins after a loss of control are thinner (in terms of time) because the airplane is aerodynamically cleaner and will accelerate to a speed outside the envelope much more quickly.

One thing the pump builder didn't do that I find curious is recommend that pumps be changed at certain intervals. For some reason, we all seem to be loath to admit that things on airplanes wear out, and that replacement before they wear out is an important part of maintaining the airplane and keeping the wolves at bay. If the airplane has one air pump, for example, regardless of the backups installed, it doesn't seem smart to just run that one pump until it fails. Personally, I change the primary pump once a year, which is about every 500 hours.

Mags and alternators seem to follow about the

16 same cycle as vacuum pumps, so these are also on a 500-hour cycle.

CHECKLISTS

If something on the airplane breaks, there is an emergency checklist to use. Depending on the airplane, this covers everything from ditching to dealing with an opened door in flight. Early on, we learn the simple fact that some of these should be committed to memory. The ones that deal with sudden things, like engine or system failures, are good lists to store in your noggin because when it all goes silent there might not be time to retrieve and read a checklist. On the other hand, ditching is probably not something that most pilots would commit to memory, because most of us spend very little time flying over water. In the pressurized airplane that I fly most of the time, the list that covers cabin air contamination is important, as is the one on how to deal with a sudden decompression of the cabin.

There are checklists for normal operation, too, and use of these is important. Sure, if you fly the same airplane all the time, you should know all the things that need to be done before takeoff or before landing. But that is not the point. The point is that the use of the checklist insures that nothing is left undone—ever.

I can remember two cases in which I was riding in the back seat of a Bonanza. The pilots in front did not use a checklist, and had I not been suspicious and pointed out that the trim was still nose-up from landing, the airplane would have left the ground in a hard-to-manage trim state. In both cases the pilots were experienced Bonanza pilots, and I'm sure they felt they knew the airplane well enough not to use a checklist. But facts are facts, and any pilot might overlook a cru-

cial item if the preparations don't follow the methodical   **17**
manner that is dictated by the use of a checklist. Airline
pilots use them, corporate pilots use them, military pilots use them. General aviation pilots don't have to use
them, but it is foolish not to use a checklist.

AND CHECK RIDES

Like checklists, check rides are methodical examina-
tions of certain things that are related to safe flying.
Everyone who learns to fly and earns a private license
takes at least one check ride. In the good old days,
almost all check rides were given by FAA inspectors,
employees of the FAA (or CAA in the past); now virtually all check rides are given by examiners designated
by the FAA to perform this service.

There is an art to learning how to take a check ride.
It is just another part of learning to fly. There is no
question that most pilots are a touch nervous on a check
ride. Some more than others. This isn't all bad, because
with some nervousness, the check ride can become a
look at the pilot's ability to compensate for an adverse
factor. Maybe there is no question that the pilot can, on
a pretty day, go out and do all the requisite items for the
ride. Maybe they can be done perfectly when solo, or
with a good-buddy instructor by your side. But intro-
duce an ogre into the cockpit, a person who can decide
whether you emerge triumphant or defeated, and the
atmosphere changes. The check ride items are relatively simple and if a pilot can't do them with an unsettling influence at his side, then the licensing system has
served its purpose. We shouldn't want to exercise the
privileges of a certificate if nervousness forces excessive errors in flying.

Every check ride can be a memorable experience;

18   a couple stand out as good learning events for me.

The first was my original ATP ride, only they called it the ATR, airline transport rating, at that time. This was in 1958, and at that time only FAA inspectors in the air carrier branch were authorized to give check rides for the ATR. I was working in Little Rock, Arkansas, at the time, flying a Twin Bonanza, and my checker was J. J. Werbke of the FAA's Fort Worth office. That was before the days of "cost-effectiveness" because Werbke made a special trip from Fort Worth to Little Rock just to administer this one check ride.

We spent most of the morning on the oral exam. A Trans-Texas Airways captain had helped me prepare, and the emphasis he put on the oral exam had me ready. I had memorized every known fact about the Twin Bonanza. Oil pressure or tire pressure—it was all stored and ready. When we finished with that, Werbke looked out the window and said that we could fly when the weather cleared. I said that I didn't mind doing it IFR, but he nixed that idea. In retrospect, I wonder if he wasn't trying to induce a bit of uncertainty.

The weather cleared after lunch and off we went. Everything went well on the ride, but there is one item that stands out. While flying in preparation for the ride, my mentor had stressed the fact that it would be better to be a little bit slow getting something done than to make a mistake. In the warm cockpit of the twin (it was July in Arkansas) I had managed to be methodical. Then, as we were partway through a maneuver that I remember as a "canyon approach," a descending, turning, climbing contortion that emulated a letdown into a canyon and then a retreat, Werbke pulled an engine. I knew that was coming and had practiced it.

Usually, if in a turn when an engine failure is given, the drill is to roll level and then go into the procedures

to identify and secure the dead engine. But if you roll **19**
level while in the canyon, splat, all over the canyon
wall. So the turn was continued until on the safe exit
heading. Then I went into the business of securing the
engine. Dead foot, dead engine. I have forgotten which
engine it was, but for the first time on the ride I was
having trouble with the thought process and, initially, I
misidentified the dead engine. My hand started toward
the power quadrant, and if you can feel a stare I could
feel Werbke's eyes on my hand. My motions must have
been tentative enough to make him suspect that something notable was about to happen. Then I realized that
mental paralysis had set in and said, "Self, stop. Sort
this out before you do anything." I did, and the story
had a happy ending. In tribute to the inspector's power
of observation, though, he did mention the engine-out
procedure in the debriefing. As I recall, he said that he
was all but convinced that I was reaching for the wrong
lever and he was glad that I got it right. So was I.

FAILED AIRSPEED

All check rides have lessons; the other one offered here
was for the single-engine ATP, some years after the ride
just related. This flight was in a Cessna 172 with John
Doster, an FAA inspector with the longest and most
distinguished career of all. It was a winter day, gray and
overcast, but the ceiling was high enough for what we
were doing.

All the required maneuvers were completed and
then Doster had me go through one of his favorite drills.
Intercept an outbound bearing from an NDB and then
fly that until intercepting the localizer at Allentown,
Pennsylvania. Then finish the ride with a well-executed
ILS and you win. I have seen him give the ride in multi-

20 engine airplanes and then it's always on one engine. As the 172 was maneuvered for the ILS, I wondered what he'd do to liven up the proceedings.

As we continued, a little rain started going pitty-pat on the windshield. From under the hood, I asked if it was still good VFR, or did we need a clearance? He said the ceiling was still high and the visibility good. As we continued, I sensed that something was wrong. It sounded like we were going fast, but the airspeed was sinking. Wind shear? There wasn't any on departure. Then I became convinced that Doster had come up with some devious means of disabling the airspeed. It was raining, and if the airplane had had pitot heat I guess I would have turned it on. But it had no heat.

Disregarding the airspeed, I continued the approach to the decision height and looked up—to a windshield that was almost opaque. The rain I heard was freezing rain and the pitot head was simply iced over. When I asked Doster why he didn't tell me, he said that we needed to get on the ground as quickly as possible, and what we were doing would accomplish just that. And he laughed and said he wanted to see what I would do about the airspeed.

ALL WEATHER

Once the basics of flying are learned, one of the finest challenges is in learning more about the relationship of weather to flying. The fact that this is both a simple and a complex relationship makes it all the more interesting.

Let's look at the simple part first.

What you see is what you get in weather. Regardless of the forecast or the *Farmer's Almanac,* the weather that exists is fact. Where pilots tend to destroy the simplicity of the matter is in trying to wish the

weather into some other form, perhaps into the form
that was forecast. It often is not easy to accept simple
facts when you think something should be more complicated.

A good example of this came in December 1986,
when relatively rare fog blanketed the central and
southeastern U.S. for days.

The facts of the matter were plain. There was a
strong temperature inversion and warmer air over cold
is a good fogmaker. Also, the upper-air patterns were
stable. There was a straight east-west flow which pre-
cludes the development of strong surface weather systems that would result both in wind to blow the fog
away and mixing of air to lessen the effects of the inversion. So the fog was there and it was dense.

But a lot of pilots wouldn't accept the simple fact,
and one morning in the Kansas City area I heard a
number of airplanes on the frequency, waiting for the
weather at Kansas City to come up to minimums. Certainly it would eventually, but none of these lads had
that much fuel in their tanks and, one by one, they had
to accept the fact of the matter and hustle off to Lincoln,
Nebraska, the closest place with minimums.

In this same time period, I heard a few pilots at-
tempting the ultimate folly at Charleston, West Virginia. The airport there was socked in, with runway
visual range below 1,000 feet and the reported visibility
at ¹⁄₁₆ of a mile. It is legal for pilots operating under Part
91 of the regulations (not for hire) to "have a look," and
indeed it might be legal for them to land regardless of
the report if they have the approach lights or runway in
sight at the decision height. On this foggy morning, two
pilots were, on a continuing basis, trying to get into
Charleston. The fact was that given the conditions,
there would be no way to complete the approach with-

22 out cheating. And the record has shown this brand of cheating to be lethal. Regardless of the forecast, the weather was too bad to land.

ALL WEATHER CHANGES

Things like widespread fog are simple matters because they are the product of a stable and easily identified condition. Weather becomes much more complex when it is related to a rapidly developing weather system. It's still true that what you see is what you get, but what you see can change rapidly and the pilot's challenge becomes one of rolling with the punches.

My trip was from New Jersey to Florida, with a fuel stop at Myrtle Beach, S.C. The weather had been worse than forecast all along the way, and the weather at Myrtle was at minimums where it was forecast to be much better. The airport that was my alternate for Myrtle, based on forecasts, was zero-zero, so of necessity the plan was changed from minute to minute.

On the ground at Myrtle, a conversation with the FSS revealed that there was rain to the south, but they were not expecting anything worse. Off I went. Within 45 minutes the controller broadcast a sigmet that called for, among other things, tornadoes along the route of flight. A complex weather system was developing rapidly. These things happen and a pilot who professes to be surprised by such an event doesn't understand weather. "How," you might ask, "could all the information available suggest benign conditions and then, suddenly, change to indicate that nature is about to dish out its most violent product?" It's simple. While weather information might be computerized, the atmosphere is not. It reserves the right to rearrange itself rapidly.

Something different stands out to every pilot; these are some of the things that I have long remembered in the continuing quest not only to learn to fly, but to learn as much about flying as possible.

Some other things stand out. One is that you learn as much about yourself as about flying along the way, because flying is a uniquely individual experience. On first solo, I realized quickly that it was between me and the airplane. It has been thus since, and to me it's been a fine challenge.

How do you feel after shooting an approach to minimums? How you feel tells you something about yourself. If you feel satisfied, that is good only if the approach was a good one. If you are satisfied simply with getting the job done, regardless of how sloppily it was done, worse things might be around the corner. If you maneuver an airplane through an area of questionable weather and think, whew, that was close, the implication is that you don't manage risks, you take risks.

If you make a bad landing and don't think through all the factors that contributed to the thumpy arrival, you aren't taking advantage of experience to improve. The continuous business of learning about flying can be related to another activity that is even more rewarding, if not as unique. That is the fine art of raising kids, where you spend the original years learning how to do it, and the following years expanding knowledge and sharing experience—just as we do with airplanes. I'll share with you something written on the margin of my flight log as I flew along in late 1986 when both these subjects were very much on my mind as our youngest was about to set off on his own a few days later:

24   Learning to fly is like raising kids. The objective is to be ever better at it—even after you have allegedly finished learning/raising—and to be able to look back with some satisfaction at having accomplished it with as little trouble as possible. And to remember that, with both airplanes and kids, what comes next counts for more than what has transpired.

2

Learning the Lessons

NCE YOU LEARN enough about flying to handle the airplane, the next step is the satisfying business of learning to get the most out of the airplane. For most pilots, this means traveling. It matters not whether you travel for business or personal reasons, the airplane is a fine way to go.

Much has been made of how flying saves money because time is money. Maybe there are circumstances where it does save a few bucks, but that's not really the way to think about flying. And it shouldn't be compared with riding on airliners from either a time or expense standpoint. Personal airplanes are to airliners as cars are to busses. There is a world of difference between traveling in your own conveyance and using mass transportation, whether on the ground or in the air. From every standpoint the airplane relates to the automobile. Viewed like this it is easier to keep things in perspective.

I can honestly say that I have always used my

26   airplanes as all-purpose traveling machines. Whether on magazine business or on my own business, no thought is given to using any other form of transportation. And I pay the same amount to fly on my business that my employer reimburses me to fly on company business. The airplane isn't used because it is cheap, it is used because it is, to me, the best means of transportation available.

But is it reliable? The answer to that is an unqualified yes.

THE KEY IS IFR

There is one requirement for an airplane to be a good all-purpose traveling machine. It has to be used IFR. Instrument flying is the key to minimizing the risks of weather as well as to getting where you want to go more or less when you want to get there.

Instrument flying for me goes back to 1955, the year I got my instrument rating. At that time I owned a Piper Pacer, purchased from my father for a very nepotistic sum. It was equipped for IFR, and I set out to learn about the business of flying in the clouds.

In the beginning I made a mistake that many repeat to this day. Sure, I had an instrument rating and sure, the airplane was equipped for instrument flying. But when the weather was decent, I still flew VFR—even to the point of scud-running instead of flying on instruments. IFR was something to be held at arm's length, to be used only when necessary.

The IFR of the fifties was different from today's, and perhaps that's why it was avoided when possible. There was no radar and separation was based on position reporting from pilots who were IFR. Communicating was done through what later became the flight service station, though in that day it was an INSAC, which stood for interstate airways communication station. No radar meant nobody to ask about thunderstorms or anything else. In fact, there was no weather radar system for the country then, so thunderstorms were scoped out using forecasts, weather reports, and the stability index which gave somewhat of an idea about the likelihood of puffy clouds turning into cumulonimbus.

Much of the airspace in the U.S. was uncontrolled, and unless you were flying along on airways, you just might have company in the clouds because it was perfectly legal to fly in clouds in uncontrolled airspace without a clearance. In fact, when you had a clearance that covered a route with a combination of controlled and uncontrolled airspace, the clearance would specify maintaining, for example, 6,000 feet when in controlled airspace. When in uncontrolled airspace, IFR altitude was determined the same as for VFR at that time—odd for 0–89 degrees, odd plus 500 for 90–179, even for 180–269, and even plus 500 for 270–359.

EQUIPMENT OF THE DAY

The Pacer had a Narco Omnigator, which gave VOR, localizer, marker beacon, and limited communications capability. It also had an ADF, and I added a 60-channel transceiver to be able to chat more easily with the folks on the ground.

It was not so much the equipment that limited the use of the airplane for travel, it was more its speed and limited ceiling. Point the Pacer into a strong headwind and the groundspeed could drop to a very low value. Add to that the airplane's relatively limited range—it

28   was good for about four hours with a comfortable reserve—and perplexing moments could arise.

There were not a lot of ILS systems around, so the lower minimums of a localizer approach were often unavailable. Little Rock, home base for some of the time I had the Pacer, didn't have a localizer. The only approaches were a low-frequency range and a VOR, both straight in to the shortest runway of three at the airport. The length of the runway didn't bother me, but the airlines were up to Lockheed Electras before an ILS was available and they had to make a circling approach every time until that precision approach was effective. With no ILS you were basically looking for a 500-foot ceiling and a mile visibility wherever you happened to go, though some of the low-frequency range approaches had lower minimums.

OFF LIMITS

When I was in the Army, stationed at Fort Rucker, Alabama, I went to Little Rock a lot of weekends. Now this was using an airplane to its fullest, because even with a three-day pass for a long weekend we were not supposed to stray more than 250 miles from the post, and it was almost twice that far to Little Rock. I was putting a lot of faith in the reliability of transportation by general aviation airplane, as well as betting my stripes that the airplane would get me back on time. One advantage: The headwind usually slowed me down on the way out; coming back, southeastbound, I usually had a tailwind. In the 18 months I spent at Fort Rucker, the Pacer never failed to get me to the base on time.

There was usually no way to make it nonstop to

Little Rock; Meridian, Mississippi, was the usual fuel
stop. Meridian had a localizer, and the minimums were
about 400 feet. Fred Key, one of the Key brothers who
set an endurance record of 653 hours and 34 minutes in
1935 (the record still stands), was the FBO at Meridian
and he thought I was certified crazy to be flying a Pacer
in clouds. But Fred, a fine person, was a pilot from
another day and I was slowly becoming convinced that
flying IFR was the cornerstone of reducing risk while at
the same time making the airplane useful.

One trip hangs firmly in memory. The headwind
was stronger than forecast and the Meridian weather
was worse than forecast. I have forgotten what the alternate rules were at that time, but whatever had been
selected as an alternate was clearly out of reach. I had
backed myself into a corner, with no options. Land at
Meridian or else. Fortunately the ceiling inched up until
it allowed a successful approach. From that day on,
though, I put that lesson to work on a lot of flights,
making sure that there were always some options.

WHAT ARE THE RISKS?

When I was working with my father at *Air Facts* magazine, a strong interest in safety developed. One of the
things that amazed me then, and still does, is the fact
that most pilots are not aware of the real risks in flying.
If you don't know what they are, it's hard to keep them
at arm's length.

While almost all airline and corporate jet accidents
happen during takeoff or landing, a lot of general aviation airplanes being used for transportation crash en
route. Even though en route flying can seem monoto-
nous and relatively free of immediate risk, a lot of air-

30   planes are lost in this phase. Because problems here are almost unique to general aviation they deserve special consideration.

A SPECIAL CASE

An event in early 1987 brought this home. Accidents that happen to people you don't know can be studied and lessons can be learned, but when one involves a friend it is different. The accident occupies your thoughts for a lot longer, and personal knowledge of the pilot's ability leads you down many paths looking for possible causes.

It started on a Sunday morning, with a call from Mac McClellan, *Flying's* senior editor in Kansas City. "Grim news from here. Jim and Marilyn went in out in Colorado last night in the 340. Straight in. No chance."

At first I thought that he couldn't be talking about Jim Reynolds, a fine guy and a fine pilot. Reynolds did everything to minimize risks in his flying. He took regular proficiency courses, including simulator, at Flight-Safety International. An aviation medical examiner, active flight instructor, and student of all things aeronautical, Reynolds was one to analyze everything. Just a month earlier I had flown with him in the 340 from Kansas City to Waco, Texas, on a very grungy day. It was enjoyable to sit and watch him operate the airplane with a precision that comes only from practice and proficiency. Later that evening we were flying back to Kansas City in a Mooney 252, and Jim remarked that he felt better doing night IFR in his twin than in a single. Then, when we descended into the clouds, Jim reminded me to turn on the pitot heat. Always the meticulous instructor. It couldn't have been that Jim and Marilyn that Mac was talking about. But it was.

Learn from Tragedy

Months later we knew little more than what was known the next day, but a lot of us had put a lot of thought into the accident, trying to learn something from it that would help us to better use our airplanes at the lowest possible level of risk.

Jim Reynolds was flying back to Kansas City from Palm Springs. He made a fuel stop at Farmington, New Mexico, and he was back up at Flight Level 210, 21,000 feet, over eastern Colorado. Reportedly one controller noticed altitude excursions and when asked about these Reynolds said that he had "gyro problems." Shortly afterward the airplane dove vertically into the ground. One investigator said the speed must have been up around 350 knots. Even though the ground was not soft, the engines were buried 10 feet down and one person reported that it was as if the ground swallowed the airplane and the hole it made had covered it back over.

Destruction was complete but they were able to ascertain that the landing gear and flaps were up and that the airplane was apparently intact when it hit the ground. No parts were found elsewhere and the control surface counterweights were all found in the wreckage. The elevator trim jackscrew was at a limit and if it had been nose-down that would have been logical but it was apparently nose-up.

So here is a well-trained and proficient pilot flying a twin IFR at night in relatively good weather, using an airplane as it was designed to be used, and, bang, the airplane disappears off the radar scope and dives into the ground.

We tried to think of everything and it was interesting that Reynolds's doctor friends centered their atten-

32 tion on pilot incapacitation while his nondoctor pilot friends centered their attention on the airplane and its systems—specifically the autopilot–electric trim system. Nothing that we considered should be thought of as a probable, or even a possible, cause—it is all speculation in the name of education.

The Pilot

Incapacitation would likely be from one of three causes. The first would be carbon monoxide, either from a problem with the gasoline heater in the airplane or through a highly unlikely failure that would have contaminated the bleed air used to pressurize the cabin. Second would be a failure of the pressurization system, which, at 21,000 feet, would result in a loss of consciousness. Most pressurized airplanes have an on-off switch for the pressurization system that is relatively easy to neglect to turn on. But there is a red light on the annunciator panel that comes on when the cabin altitude exceeds a safe value and this would be hard to miss. Could the light have been burned out? Checklist procedures call for checking all annunciator lights as operational and Reynolds was a user of checklists. Also, the length of time they had been at 21,000 feet would be almost past the absolute limit a healthy person could retain consciousness at that altitude. And if the autopilot had been on and operating normally and the pilot passed out, the airplane wouldn't have dived into the ground as it did unless a hypoxic pilot decided the autopilot was all wrong, turned it off, and took over. The third cause could have been some physical ailment. Reynolds was a healthy guy in his forties, didn't smoke and took only an occasional drink. But others like him

have just keeled over with faulty plumbing and that is   **33**
always a possibility.

The Airplane

There isn't a likely or logical problem with the powerplants that would have led the airplane into a screaming dive at such a high speed. And if the airplane was
in one piece just before it hit, there isn't any logical
control system problem—though the possibility always
exists that something might have come off or come
loose, but wasn't found because of the complete destruction of the airplane. That leaves the electric trim
system as a possibility, with interest in it heightened by
the fact that the trim jackscrew was found at the extreme limit of travel. Trouble with that is, it was apparently nose-up, and at first it was hard to see how, with
full nose-up trim, the airplane could have hit vertically
at extremely high speed unless it was in a spiral dive.

Trim Misunderstanding

We did learn one thing about the electric trim systems
when going through all the possibilities. A lot of pilots
don't fully understand the characteristics of these systems, especially what happens and what to do when a
trim runs away.

There is a button on the control wheel that, on
some airplanes, is labelled "autopilot/electric trim disconnect." The button does disconnect the autopilot, but
it only interrupts the trim. So, for example, if an electric
trim system were to run away in a nose-down direction,
pushing the button would stop the trim, but if the button
were released, the trim would resume running again.

34   And there is no certification requirement that an airplane be controllable with full trim in either direction.

The lesson there is to learn which switch or circuit breaker can be used to remove all power from the trim system in case of a runaway, and to remember that the electric trim can be stopped, even in a runaway, simply by stopping the movement of the manual trim wheel. Then always watch closely. Those of us who fly airplanes without a full autopilot always know what is going on with trim because it doesn't move unless we move it. But with an autopilot you fly the airplane by wire, and you and all such systems are subject to malfunction. A really important part of any checkout in an airplane is the autopilot, and we should all understand all there is to know about them before flying.

SPATIAL DISORIENTATION

When thinking about the airplanes that are lost en route, while pilots are trying to get from here to there, the characteristics of a loss of control need to be considered. Why would a pilot, droning along en route, not bothered by turbulence or some other external factor, lose control? If hand flying the airplane, it could come as a result of inattention to the instruments, a result of an instrument failure or the cessation of power to some instruments because a vacuum pump failed, or because of some glitch in the electrical system.

So if an airplane is used for serious transportation the remedies are obvious. Having both standby instrumentation as well as standby power sources for instruments is an obvious aid. So is the ability to recover from an unusual attitude quickly, before it dissolves into a graveyard spiral from which recovery is unlikely. In a retractable, if there is doubt about being

in control and the airspeed is increasing rapidly, ex-   **35**
tending the landing gear and reducing the power to idle
slows the development of a true graveyard spiral and
results in lower airspeed and lower load factors in any
recovery. Unless there is some malfunction in the pitch
control portion of an autopilot or electric trim system,
a lateral loss of control (a roll) will precede a longitudi-
nal loss of control. So it stands to reason that the first
order of business is to add drag, reduce power, and roll
the wings to level, if the airspeed is high or increasing
rapidly.

Whether a loss of control is caused by some mechanical force, or because the pilot simply doesn't pay
attention to the flying, it's a cinch that the pilot becomes
spatially disoriented. That is why, in instrument training and proficiency flying, the practice of unusual attitude recoveries is so important. It is there that we can
develop the automatic, reflex procedures to apply to
any possible situation, so they will be available for use
should the bad time ever come.

MORE THAN FACE VALUE

There is perhaps more than meets the eye in recovery
from unusual attitudes and spiral dives. In trying to
better understand this phenomenon, I went flying in one
of FlightSafety International's Cessna 421 simulators. I
had the instructor fail the vacuum power system. It was
easy enough to catch the fact that the artificial horizon
on the left side had a problem. I then looked at the
horizon on the right side. It looked okay and agreed
with the turn and bank and other instruments. So I
decided to fly the right horizon and did so until I noticed
that the right vertical speed was indicating a rapidly
increasing descent. At that time I moved back to the left

36 side of the panel, where I saw that the airspeed was high and increasing rapidly, the vertical speed was pegged in a descent, and the turn and bank was full scale.

At this time I did what most pilots would probably (and wrongly) do by instinct. I pulled back on the wheel to get out of what was apparently a dive. I also started rolling in nose-up trim. This only served to tighten the spiral dive. I was unable to quickly analyze the situation and the airplane was into the ground 40 seconds after leaving 16,000 feet. The only "mistakes" I had purposely made were to assume that the problem with the left gyro was isolated, not a vacuum system failure, and to pull back on the wheel in response to the instrument readings. Either of those mistakes would be easy to make in the heat of battle. Too, doing this in the simulator involved no G loading, which would further complicate an already complicated event. The G force would build in a spiral dive and would, according to one engineer's estimate, reach as high as 5 G in a fully developed spiral. Not only would this much G force be disorienting, it could lead to unconsciousness in a relatively short time—perhaps less time than it would take to reach the ground.

What this led me to do was realize that there is a lot more to redundancy than having two vacuum pumps or two artificial horizons, and that we have to have a procedure to break a tie when two artificial horizons disagree. And, like it or not, that procedure has to involve partial panel flying—keeping the wings level with the turn and bank or turn coordinator and seeing which, if either, artificial horizon agrees with the other information on the panel.

When first getting into instrument flying I knew very little about weather, even though I once toyed with the idea of getting a degree in meteorology. I guess I knew what was required to pass the rather skimpy and unrealistic written exams of the day, but I still was surprised by weather a lot. The first northeastern U.S. coastal storm that I saw totally baffled me, as did the fact that behind a cold front it could be cloudy over the Appalachians because of lake effect, but clear over the coastal plain. Slowly, through studying weather both on the ground and while in the airplane, I started learning something about what goes on in the atmosphere. When I lived in Little Rock in the '70s, working for *Flying,* a very fine meteorologist, the late Vern Jetton, patiently helped me understand the relationship between surface weather and weather patterns aloft. If I had a specific question about the factors that had affected a flight, he'd dig out all the records from the day in question and go over them in great detail. The most excited I ever saw him was late in December when it was raining cats and dogs, and Little Rock exceeded 100 inches of rainfall in one year for the first time in history. The roof in his office was leaking into a bucket he had put on the floor but he was grinning from ear to ear, savoring weather history in the making.

To use an airplane in most weather, not increase the risks, and not be fooled, you do have to face some meteorological truths that, if ignored, can result in a big spike in risk as you use an airplane.

The forecasts that we use are based on computer models of the atmosphere. As long as the old atmosphere behaves as the computer thinks it will, then the forecasts are pretty good. How do we tell if the atmo-

38   sphere isn't behaving as anticipated? That can, in many cases, be a very logical process. The wind and temperature aloft forecasts are based on anticipated patterns, so if these forecasts are in error, then everything else is suspect. Most useful in the eastern half of the U.S. is the fact that if the wind is more southerly than forecast, or if a wind from a southerly direction is stronger than forecast, then the weather in the area is likely to be worse than forecast. Why? Because a low to the west is apparently stronger than anticipated and the warm air flowing up from the south at low level can hold more moisture. The Gulf of Mexico is an excellent moisture source. In fact, the ability of the atmosphere to hold moisture doubles with each 11° C rise in temperature.

For some of the time I lived in Little Rock I had a Skyhawk. The airplane was lavishly equipped and I used it for a lot of IFR travel, especially between Little Rock and Wichita when the airplane business there was in its heyday. The weather along the route often defied prediction and was always interesting. And there was a built-in warning of the likelihood of conditions worse than forecast. The Boston Mountains, not small hills, lined up south of the route up the Arkansas River valley. With a strong south or southwest wind there would be wave conditions north of the mountains. If the forecast had been for relatively light 3,000-foot winds but the wave was strong up near Fort Smith, watch out for bad weather later in the day.

A strong southwest wind up at the 18,000-foot level can portend severe weather, if all other conditions are ripe. Why? Because this indicates a trough of low pressure aloft to the west and the southwest wind is bearing colder air aloft over warmer air at the surface, contributing to instability.

Beware an occlusion. When a low-pressure area is

moving slowly but has a very strong circulation around 39
it, the cold front can overtake the warm front, and when
this happens instability becomes very strong. Tornadoes are often associated with occlusions, as are tre-
mendously turbulent clouds and low-level clear air
turbulence well clear of areas of electrical discharge or
precipitation.

500 MILLIBARS

The 500 mb chart, which reflects the circulation up at
the 18,000-foot level, is an important one because lows
at the surface tend to track with or parallel to the winds
at this level. And if there is a closed low aloft—that is,
a complete circulation around a low—then surface systems will move away from it very slowly, if at all, and
nothing is likely to change much until the closed low
aloft breaks up.

The business about storms tracking with the
18,000-foot winds was clearly demonstrated to me by a
hurricane one year. The hurricane had just come on the
Alabama coast as I was flying from Wichita, Kansas,
back to New Jersey. The prognosis was that it would
head northeast, get back out to sea, and then hug the
Atlantic coast, giving the New York area a big blow.

I was flying at 19,000 feet where the forecast wind
was westerly. But it was actually out of the south.
Hmmm. That means the hurricane will just become a
low-pressure storm system that will track up through
the central U.S., and there will be no strong storm in the
New York area. When I got home, my wife told me we
were about to have a hurricane. "Forget it," I said.

The next day the New York papers warned of the
approaching storm but by afternoon they too decided
that the storm wasn't coming. There was just a lot of

40 rain. So a unique insight into weather is available to any pilot. All you have to do is maintain your curiosity about what is going on up there. Because the relationship of the airplane to weather is so important, the pilot who isn't curious and doesn't bother to learn about weather might be in for a rough time.

GOING IT ALONE

When we consider that general aviation pilots often lose control of airplanes en route while airline pilots do not, and that the airline record is much better than the general aviation record, the question of a single pilot versus a crew has to be reviewed.

The business of a single pilot doing all the airborne work alone is complicated by the fact that, in many or most cases, that person is also responsible for a lot of other things, not the least of which might be the financial support of the airplane. Can a person be a consummate pilot and business executive at the same time? An airline or corporate pilot who flies every flight with help can still blow the whistle if he is worried about something or doesn't feel 100-percent fit, and the flight will still go on. A single pilot might not have this luxury. If I don't fly it, it doesn't go. Is this a factor?

Some answers lie in the way airline crews operate their airplanes. Having said in the beginning that the personal airplane should be compared with the personal automobile and not to the airliner, I have to backtrack a little here. From an economic and convenience standpoint the personal airplane does not relate to the airlines. But because we do operate in the same airport-airways system and in the same air, there is a close operational relationship and we can learn much from the way they fly.

With a crew, you have two (or three) people who are interacting on a continuous basis. There are checklists and procedures to follow, and these in themselves can help the crew put things other than flying out of mind. That might be what you call stress management. Certainly when you are performing one task but something else on your mind distracts from the primary goal, you are under stress. If you can put the detractor out of mind and concentrate wholly on the job at hand, then the stress is being managed. This would apply to any business or personal problems, or to any relatively minor physical ailments.

Years ago at an airport where I worked, the people who owned and flew airplanes maintained a close relationship with the people who worked at the FBO. This took a good turn one night when one of the customers, an accomplished pilot, had a death in his family at a city a hundred or so miles away. It was late in the day and he came to the airport to fly there. It was obvious to one of the pilots in the office that this person was under great stress. The solution was simple: fly there with him. There was no way that person who had just lost a loved one would have done a very good job of flying.

MIND MANAGEMENT

Because there is often a lot of time to think during a flight, how can a single pilot keep his mind on flying and not on personal problems or business deals? This is where we can take lessons from the way crews operate. The en route part of the flight is a time when we can make up for the fact that there is but one pilot to do the work when the action heats up, on the arrival. Procedures can be reviewed while a constant check on the airplane and its systems is maintained. Perfection can

42   be demanded in navigation, and in maintaining altitude. Do the required things, and then check them as a second pilot would. When the action heats up, during a close approach, for example, it is time for the single pilot to become a crew. Make all the altitude callouts on descent—1,000 feet to go, 500 feet to go, 100 feet to go, and reaching the assigned altitude, minimum descent altitude, or decision height. Call sink rates and airspeed on final, and carry on a running commentary about how the approach is going. I get so engrossed in an approach that it's hard to see how anyone could think about anything else at such a time, but the record shows it is a problem for some pilots some of the time.

Mind Against Weather

Dealing with weather is an important part of mind management because there's often strong pressure to get there, regardless, which in turn explains a lot of the general aviation weather accidents. Again, look at the way the airlines do it. They have dispatchers—a lot more people in on the deal—but the methodical way they manage operations can be applied to a single-pilot, single-airplane operation.

Start with low ceilings and below-minimum visibility conditions. Airliners are simply held or dispatched to an alternate when the reported visibility is below landing minimums. Flying not-for-hire, we have a different situation. We can shoot any approach we wish, and even if the reported visibility is below limits, it is often held that we can legally land if the runway or lights are in sight at the decision height. The FAA legal department takes an occasional swipe at pilots who do that, but because of the way the regulations are written, pilots often win. However, the FAA can be in a much

more aggressive mode on FAR violations, so pilots are   43
well-advised to cross the *t* and dot the *i* on every approach, which would suggest not beginning one if the
reported visibility is below limits.

But why would a general aviation pilot, probably
with less training and perhaps with less equipment,
even want to shoot an approach that would be denied
an airline crew? Probably just because it is allowed.
Indeed, there was a tragic case of an airline captain
flying a light airplane into a major airport, shooting an
approach with the runway visual range below limits,
and crashing into a taxiing airliner. If it's below limits,
it's below limits and the wise general aviation pilot
dispatches himself to another location to await improvement. There are some who say "why not take a
look," but this is really pushing the practical use of an
airplane to extremes.

AT MINIMUMS OR NO REPORTING

The weather at Dallas Love was well below forecast at
300 obscured, with a mile and a half visibility in fog. Out
at the big airport, D/FW, the weather had really gone
to pot. They were 100 obscured and a half a mile, with
runway visual range that was below the minimums of
some users. The controller sounded like he thought
Love might further fold before we got there. There were
nine airplanes being lined up for the approach to Love
and my 210 was one of the slower ones. The controller
kept egging us on for speed and I could tell from watching my area navigation system that the turn onto final
would be close to the marker.

Patrick Bradley, with whom I collaborated on the
book *Instrument Flying Refresher,* was flying, and I
was carefully watching him put together the pieces of

44   the puzzle. There was some wind shear so the approach would be bumpy, and it would have to be flown fast. And I told him with conviction that if we missed this approach, we would go back to Texarkana. To me, close approaches are like gunfights at the O.K. Corral: If you miss with the first shot, you don't get another chance.

Down we came, maintaining a lot of speed in honor of the Learjet that was sniffing our path. The lights hove into view just before time to call a missed approach. I hated to do it because it probably wouldn't have been necessary, but when the flaps were applied to slow the airplane down a little, I applied the necessary forward pressure on the wheel to keep from ballooning back up into the murk. Had that happened, we'd have been off for Texarkana.

There is one exception to dispatch rules and weather—that is airports where weather is not reported. This is something to do with care. So done, it does not entail any unusual risk. The key is in trying to seek unofficial information about the weather, from a Unicom frequency for example. Because most of these are nonprecision approaches, you'd want a Unicom operator to say the weather is pretty good before using the fuel to shoot an approach. Certainly if the person said he couldn't see the hangar for the fog, it would not be wise to try. If the approach is conducted, staying on the safe side means adhering strictly to the approach procedures and not starting a descent from the minimum descent altitude until and unless the runway is in sight.

JUGGLING

The key to this is in wearing three hats, in looking at the weather in three different ways. The dispatcher has to

question whether he wants to release the flight and take **45**
the responsibility for it being an operation that involves
as little risk as possible. The captain has to be satisfied
that the dispatcher isn't taking unnecessary risks in his
behalf, and the copilot has to help the captain keep the
risk low and alert him to any straying from the straight
and narrow. You can do all those things for yourself.

IF YOU DON'T LIKE IT, DON'T DO IT

Some of the best pilots I know shy completely away
from weather flying, and there is nothing wrong with
this. Airplanes are just plain fun to fly, and if a pilot's
choice is to fly for the sake of flying as opposed to going
somewhere, fine. Some I know simply do not feel comfortable with their ability to judge weather, to operate
the airplane in clouds, or to accommodate the demands
of the air traffic control system. Our present level of
training often does not do much to help a pilot with any
of those things. Weather education might be limited to
that required to pass the FAA written test, which is
woefully inadequate. Some instructors shy away from
training flights in actual IFR conditions. And I have
flown with instrument-rated pilots who never talked to
or dealt with an FAA radar facility in the course of their
IFR training.

I remember one day watching a relatively new instrument-rated pilot shoot an ILS approach that you
never would have seen in an FAA-minimum training
curriculum. The controller was vectoring him for the
approach, and was badgering us to keep the speed up
for as long as possible. That meant leaving the landing
gear and approach flaps stowed until fairly late in the
approach. They were extended after we were inside the
outer marker, and the combination of the hustle and all

46   the trim changes of flaps extension and slowing were more than this pilot could take. He said, "They can't make you do that." No, they can't make you do anything. But if we are to fit our airplanes into busy airports, we have to learn to do things like that—and they can be done quite safely by a pilot with practice.

AHHHHHHHCHOOO, OR WHY DID I DO THAT?

There are stresses to flying other than those dealing with airplanes, weather, and controllers. The stresses of business or personal problems that might interact with flying have to be managed, and the key here is a totally professional approach to flying. In the same category are the very real stresses of feeling slightly below par, whether it be from a cold or a self-inflicted wound the night before the morning of the flight. Anything that might divert your attention has to be considered.

There is a fine line here because a lot of accidents have probably occurred due to pilot incapacitation, or inability to act, because of a relatively mild physical problem or mental diversion that could not be established after the fact. I have had letters from pilots describing "anxiety" attacks that sounded like hyperventilation. The cause of that is rapid breathing, which results in excess loss of carbon dioxide and can bring on lightheadedness, tingling of the extremities, palpitation, muscle spasms, and even fainting. You wouldn't want to go flying with a person who is about to do all those things. But if you take a cold flying, for example, and decide after takeoff that the cold is worse than you thought it was and become anxious about continuing the flight, you might go into that rapid breathing syndrome. Carried far enough, it could wipe

you out. At the very least, your mind would focus on the
symptoms, and it's a good bet that for the duration of
the flight you would be thinking more about the cold
and the giddiness than about the flight. And that is the
type of stress that can kill in airplanes.

Perhaps the best question to ask yourself about an
ailment or state of mind is whether or not you can put
it out of mind and go about your business. If the answer
is uncertain, then the outcome of the flight might be
likewise.

SNOWSTORM VERSUS BUSINESS TURMOIL

I went through a good example of this one day in early
November. I was supposed to go to Washington to talk
to a flight instructor's group that evening. The plan was
to leave about 3:30 P.M., anticipating some air traffic
delay, to arrive in Washington at 5:15. I've done that
many times. Later in the evening, about nine, I would fly
back home. That's a little trick that you can do in a
general aviation airplane.

The trouble this day was that there were a lot of
other factors working. The first was the weather. It was
cold and rainy with worse conditions threatened. I must
have run off 50 pages from the weather services that
operate through CompuServe, gathering every possible
bit of data. It looked okay for the trip down. There were
no reports of icing except at high levels, and a good
picture of the below-10,000-foot weather was at hand.
There would be some low-level turbulence, but the forecasts and trends in current weather indicated that the
airport would be comfortably above ILS landing minimums. There were plenty of good alternates to the
south, at least according to the forecasts. A negative

48   was that the temperature at Trenton, home base, had dropped to 32, and what had been reported as rain on all the previous sequences changed to "ice pellets." I checked air traffic delays and they were not too bad, though they would surely get worse closer to the rush hour. Still, the trip there was a "go" with the only negative possibility that of being late because of an excessive air traffic delay.

Enter the rest of the picture. We had had a lot of recent changes in our business. Some of these had occupied about 100 percent of my thinking time for several days, as I searched for a solution to a difficult problem. The day after the Washington trip an important meeting was scheduled, one that I absolutely positively did not want to miss. The forecast for later in the evening did not project weather below minimums, but it did call for snow. When it starts snowing all bets are off. How would the cross-section of the atmosphere change for ice? What if freezing rain started to fall while the airplane was on the ground at Washington? Could I get it deiced? If the weather soured, was there any way to make the meeting other than my little airplane?

All the time I was thinking about these things, I was also thinking about business. Did I want to go flying with a person whose mind was racing on other subjects? Never before had I not had confidence in my ability to set all things aside for the enjoyment of a challenging flight: the final decision was not to go. I sure didn't want to provide a solution by plopping into the Potomac River because I was thinking about something else. It turned out to be a good decision for other reasons: that evening snow started, and Washington was smothered by a record snowfall, which would likely have had a bearing on my return trip, whether by airplane, airline, or Amtrak. Sorry I didn't get there, folks.

I usually make it, but there were just too many things   **49**
working.

DEMON RUM

There have been all manner of experiments on the effects of alcohol on flying performance. In a fairly controlled experiment, a couple of us tackled a Learjet simulator stone sober, after one drink, and then after a lot of drinks. The results were revealing. We did okay at the mechanics of flying sober, made some stupid mistakes after one drink, and thought we did a great job but actually did very poorly after drinks and dinner and wine and brandy. The scary thing, though, was that we did not crash while flying a relatively demanding airplane through visual and low IFR approaches and frequently practiced emergencies with a snootfull. The reason this is scary is that there are undoubtedly pilots out there who fly after drinking, and they tend to get away with this practice. And they will probably continue to get away with it until some untoward event occurs. In our little experiment we survived, but had there been an unusual emergency, or wind shear, or something demanding like having to interpret the weather radar and avoid a thunderstorm cell in the terminal area, we would have most certainly failed.

There has also been research on flying with a hangover, and this has to be treated in the same way as minor physical ailments. If the aftereffects of booze are such that you give thought to them and can't put them out of mind, then you shouldn't fly. In any and every case a pilot has to be able to put 100 percent into the activity.

50 STANDARD OPERATING PROCEDURE

One of the other things corporate flight operations do that adds order to their movements is follow standard operating procedures. I know a lot of people think that heaping procedures on top of procedures might hamper the use of an airplane, but when something reduces risk it means you have a better chance of achieving good use while at the same time staying alive, and that has to be the primary objective.

One of my favorite SOPs for the past ten years has been to always fly IFR. Some of the readers of *Flying* magazine take this to mean that I think VFR is beneath my dignity, but this is far from the case. As the company that owned our magazine grew larger, and when the magazine was sold to an even larger company, the responsibilities attendant to our use of airplanes increased. And if any one thing will strike fear into the hearts of the management of a publicly held company, it would be the thought of an employee flying a light airplane colliding with an airliner. We purchased enough insurance to cover that, but in order to keep the premium reasonable it was our job to keep the risk of such a collision as low as possible.

To me that meant IFR operation, where the FAA is responsible for separation of all participating airplanes. All airliners participate, so that takes care of them. I also happen to personally feel that it is the individual pilot's responsibility to the 240 million citizens who are not pilots to do everything possible to minimize the risk of collisions between light airplanes and airliners. I have had too much fun using airplanes for the past 36 years to want to see the privilege compromised because a pilot in a small airplane is involved in a collision with an airliner.

Other SOPs include avoiding intersection takeoffs   **51**
if at all possible, exceeding the FAA required minimum
fuel for any flight by at least 15 minutes, never going into
the last hour of fuel in the airplane except in emergency,
not flying past 10 P.M. unless accompanied by another
current pilot, and always engaging in some form of
proficiency flying each year.

I always calculate the required runway length for
my single if that available is less than 3,500 feet, if the
temperature is in excess of ISA plus 10, if the field
elevation is above 2,000 feet, or if the airplane is flying
at more than 90 percent of its gross weight. It almost
goes without saying that thunderstorms are avoided by
at least five miles, twenty if severe storms are forecast.
And even though my present airplane has deicing that
is approved for flight in icing conditions, that equipment
is used only to get rid of ice accumulated as I extract the
airplane from any icing that is encountered.

If you are flying an airplane without deicing or
radar, the SOP on icing and thunderstorms would need
to change to something a bit more conservative. Some,
flying airplanes less stable in roll than the 210 I fly,
might want to require at least a functional wing-leveler
autopilot if the flight is going to be in instrument
meteorological conditions. If flying a twin, you might
want minimum runway lengths for accelerate-stop or
go, and a lot of single pilots might want higher than
minimum weather.

RESULTS AND REWARDS

Going back to the beginning—that Pacer in 1955—and
flying forward to today, what have the results been?
Quite good, thank you, with the best results obtained in
the Cessna P210. In fact, at the time this airplane turned

52 4,000 hours I had made an outright weather-only cancellation of just one flight. And that day a stop was scheduled where my mother-in-law lives, so one wag said that cancellation did not count. The 210's altitude capability (in comfort) coupled with deicing, radar, and a Stormscope give answers to a lot of questions that I always had in other airplanes.

On icing, for example: When flying without deice capability, there were only a few times when I encountered significant ice, but quite a number of flights were cancelled because ice was in the forecast. The deicing equipment has not been used a lot, certainly not in real anger more than 10 or 12 times, and most of the times the flight would have been completed without the equipment. The radar and Stormscope are larger contributors, because they have always made it possible to find a way around thunderstorms and have kept me from getting too close to anything excessively turbulent. This sure doesn't mean you fly where you want when you want; it often means a delay or a diversion involving hundreds of miles. But that is okay.

There is great satisfaction in using an airplane for transportation. There are not a lot of enjoyable outdoor challenges left in the world for those of us who don't race boats, cars, or airplanes, and this certainly ranks right at the top. Only in boats do you have the relationship with wind and weather that we have in airplanes, and perhaps that is why so many pilots (I'm one) greatly enjoy sailboats.

Take a day when the ceiling and visibility are at minimum, throw in some en route challenges like thunderstorms to avoid and ice to deal with, and add a few busted forecasts. The challenge is to deliver the goods without turbulence, without adding risk, and landing

with more fuel than the law requires. All that means you   53
have to do it just right—just as you have to straighten
up and sail right on a day when the wind is gusting past
30 knots at the lake. Each takes your undivided attention and if you ever find yourself thinking about something else while sailing or flying, it's time for a checkup.

3

The Airplanes

OVER THE YEARS it has been my privilege to fly more than 200 different types of airplanes, many for evaluation in the three magazines for which I have worked. To do this I had to develop a means of relating to the airplanes. What I did was to first analyze what the airplane is and what it is supposed to do. Then I tried to put myself in the position of the owner or operator of the airplane. Up to a certain point this was relatively easy to do, because at one point or another I had owned or leased a number of different types of general aviation airplanes. If it was a Skyhawk, for example, the airplane had to be considered in the context of basic four-place airplanes, and because I had owned a couple of those that was simple enough. Context: It's a given that the airplane is slower than a Bonanza, for example, and frustration is the only result when you fly a Skyhawk and think the whole time about an airplane that will go 40 knots faster.

After being exposed to the world's fastest civilian

airplane, Concorde, I learned that when flying anything
short of that airplane, you do have to put speed in context. I was on Concorde's flight deck one night, and
when I saw some lights pass beneath I asked a crewmember if that was one of their 747s headed in the other
direction. No, not really, it was a 747 going in the same
direction. The captain reminded me that Concorde is
700 knots faster than a 747 and from that moment on I
knew that there is only one truly fast airplane; the rest
involve compromise.

THE BASICS

The basic airplanes offer a unique combination of flying
and affordability. At least they are more affordable
than more complex airplanes. When I had my Pacer
back in the '50s, I could cash a check for a hundred
bucks and go on a long trip, paying cash for gas along
the way. When I had my Skyhawk in the '70s the price
of fuel had escalated mightily, but the airplane still
moved around on a relatively inexpensive basis. Are
they capable? Well, a Cessna Skyhawk penetrated the
air defenses of the Soviet Union and its 19-year-old
pilot landed the aircraft in Red Square. You can't get
much more capable than that.

My P210 cost a lot more to fly than my Pacer or
Skyhawk, but in return it offered more, which is another
way of saying that each airplane has its assets. I recall
a Texan friend once saying that you could make better
time in west Texas in a fast car than in a Skyhawk. But
you wouldn't be flying in that fast car.

I had the chance to see my old Pacer in 1987, at
Lansing, Michigan, and it brought back a lot of fond
memories. I did a lot of things with that little airplane,
including spending one of my longest days aloft. It was

56 a December flight from Linden, New Jersey, to Little Rock, Arkansas. The day at Linden got off to a bad start because, for some reason, the engine wouldn't start of its own accord. The line crewman on duty was a huge fellow, and when he propped the Pacer, he put more spin on the prop than the starter could manage when it was working. We took off at 7:30, had a fierce headwind, and after stops at Martinsburg and Charleston, West Virginia; Bowling Green, Kentucky; and Memphis, Tennessee, we landed in Little Rock at midnight. Not a lot of distance, only about 900 nautical miles, but a lot of hours. A faster airplane would have made it sooner, but a car would have been slower. The old Pacer took me to court, to my marriage and honeymoon, and when I was in the Army, it took me on a lot of fun trips.

Despite the fondness of those memories, the Skyhawk was my favorite basic airplane. Mine was a '74 model—that was the year they planned to build 2,500 of the airplanes, and would have if the Arab oil embargo had not intervened. Some nice improvements were made to the airplane that year and I splurged and had a custom instrument panel installed along with a complete selection of the latest in King radio equipment—including a telephone. The whole purpose was to see if a basic airplane with the latest in avionics would make a viable traveling machine. The results were good. The Hawk did everything it was supposed to do and while there were occasional very slow trips, on balance the 120-knot airplane worked as an all-purpose traveling machine over the 300-nautical-mile trips that were my average at that time.

One thing an airplane like a Hawk does not do is help you maintain your proficiency in more complex airplanes. In a way, for a lot of pilots, the simplicity that results in this is good. While most pilots like to rush into

ever more complex airplanes as fast as ability and fi-   **57**
nances allow, sticking with a basic airplane for a while
helps develop other skills. If a pilot is working into IFR,
a basic airplane allows more attention to be focused on
learning weather and how to fit into the air traffic control system. The airplane also moves more slowly, allowing more time to think. The same navigational and
air traffic control tasks have to be done in flying from
Dayton to Columbus in a Learjet or in a Skyhawk. It's
obvious that in the jet you would have to think a lot
faster because a lot is compressed into less time. And
the airplane is more complex to boot.

It is possible to learn a lot about weather when
chugging around the country in a basic airplane. Living
in Little Rock and doing a lot of business in Wichita, I
got to match the little airplane against the crazy
weather that develops between those two points and, in
so doing, I learned a lot of the basic lessons about
weather.

One trip stands out has having a complete combination of ingredients. It was springtime, and there was
a low-pressure storm system to the south and southwest of my route of flight. There was some activity on
radar, but there was absolutely no static on the low-
frequency receiver that I used to listen to the tran-
scribed weather broadcast. At the time I had the luxury
of having a T-hangar that was in close proximity to the
Weather Bureau office, so I popped in there and looked
at their radar before takeoff. It looked okay on the 300-
degree bearing that would take me to Wichita.

The air at 6,000 was not smooth but not big bumpy,
and the airplane was skipping along at a higher groundspeed than anticipated. That was the good news. The
bad news was in the knowledge that when they missed
on the wind forecast, they probably missed on the ter-

58 minal forecasts. And the ones I had written down were as bad as they could be and still allow a legal flight, with an alternate. Along the way I spent a lot of time talking to controllers and flight service specialists about weather because there was some around. But neither thunder nor ice harassed this flight, and Wichita was a comfortable 600 overcast and five miles visibility when I landed at 10:15, on time for my 10:30 appointment.

I was there to fly another airplane for evaluation, and on that flight we found some ice from 5,000 feet on up where I had had none on my inbound flight at 6,000. This added a whole new set of concerns for the trip home that afternoon. A bit later, at the FSS, the radar looked okay to the southeast and, because of the possibility of ice, I filed for 4,000 feet. That was the wrong altitude for the direction of flight but the thought of ice on a Skyhawk makes you do things like that.

There was snow but no ice at 4,000 feet, so I felt okay about the flight. I was flying toward lower terrain and warmer air for the first 100 miles, and Tulsa would be a haven if it appeared wise to stop. Things continued to be acceptable to Fort Smith, which has the last ILS approach before Little Rock. When the weather is as inclement as it was this day, passing that last ILS before base does involve some commitment.

It took thought. Little Rock was reporting 200 overcast and two miles visibility in moderate rain and fog. The wind was the worst part—070 degrees at 20 with gusts to 35. According to Flight Service, the rain started about 40 miles from Little Rock and was moving to the northeast. Because I was between layers in smooth air, because it was an hour flying on to Little Rock, and because I could go there and still have enough fuel to fly back to Fort Smith, I kept the pointed spinner headed toward home. I did make the decision not to fly direct

because that was over rough terrain. Flying an airway
that went a bit north of a direct line kept my Skyhawk
over a wide valley.

The wind had lessened when I got close to home,
and it appeared that I could complete the Rnav approach to my home base, North Little Rock, instead of
the ILS to Adams Field. I asked the approach controller
to ask the tower controller if he could see an apartment
house that is three miles away from the tower and near
North Little Rock—that usually defined minimums for
the Rnav approach. He could, and the approach was
relatively easy. The lesson? In this case it was that even
on a potentially stormy day, the IFR risks in a basic
airplane can be managed.

At the time of this flight I had flown the Hawk about
1,000 hours on 427 cross-country legs. In that time I had
to cancel six trips—five for weather and one for an
engine problem caused by using 100-octane fuel in an
engine designed for 80-octane fuel. Five flights were
delayed substantially, but were flown on the day
planned. And, to show the benefits of IFR even in a
simple airplane, 94 of the 427 legs flown would have
been difficult or impossible, and certainly dangerous, to
fly VFR.

There might be a drawback to the basic airplane in
that it could invite a certain complacency. I have heard
people say that a Skyhawk or Warrior is like a rocking
chair. Maybe, but no rocking chair that I know of goes
120 knots and adds the dimension of height, making
possible very sudden stops. Some risks are indeed reduced when you fly a basic airplane. The landing speed
would be lower in case of an off-airport landing and the
chances of recovering from a loss of control without
damaging anything would be better. Put another way,
the chances of losing control would be less in a basic

60 airplane than in a slick retractable. But the basic risk of flying is not eliminated just because the airplane is simple and docile.

The mechanical simplicity of a basic airplane works in its favor, too. Simpler means less things to go wrong. It often is amazing how some people will amass a complex collection of machinery and then expect everything to work all the time. When you think of the number of separate items in a complex airplane that are subject to failure, it is almost a wonder that we ever get one going with everything working perfectly.

WEATHER IN THE BASICS

Some elements of weather have a much greater effect on operations in basic airplanes than in faster ones. Wind is the most obvious. Even though my frequent trips to Wichita from Little Rock involved only 300 miles, it wasn't always possible to do this nonstop even with the large 48 gallon tanks in the Hawk. A lot of days I would have to stop in Tulsa to fill up so I could maintain both a fuel reserve and a legal alternate.

Ceiling is another consideration. The basic airplanes aren't effective at a density altitude above 11,000 feet even when you are solo, and trying to work them in high and hot conditions just isn't rewarding.

There can be times when even lower altitudes are a problem in basics. I was flying IFR in my Hawk one day, headed from Wichita back to Little Rock, when I flew into some very heavy rain. The Kansas City center controller with whom I was talking was a friend. He noticed that the progress of my Hawk across his scope slowed markedly when I flew into the rain and he asked if everything was okay. There was a lot of subsidence (settling air) in the area and when flying in heavy rain that model Skyhawk had a requirement for full carburetor heat and less than full-throttle operation (and thus a power loss); the result was a drop in indicated speed to about 80 knots if the altitude was to be maintained. I was at 7,000 feet to start with, and finally requested a lower altitude in order to maintain a higher speed in the descent and thus fly out of the rain area more quickly.

Only once did I fly the Hawk to relatively high country—to Albuquerque. That was in the summertime and was a reminder that you can't stay in smooth air over high country in one of these airplanes on a hot afternoon. The ride into Albuquerque was indeed uncomfortable.

In 1960 I flew a basic airplane all the way across the country, and that trip, in one of the first Cherokees, has always been a pleasant memory. It was a ferry trip from the Piper factory at Vero Beach, Florida, out to Hillsboro, Oregon, which is a Portland suburb. I took three days to make the trip, stopping overnight in Tulsa and in Helena, Montana. It was VFR all the way because the airplane was hardly equipped for IFR flying, and while the weather wasn't good, it was flyable without substantial delay. The locals helped a lot, too, with the sage advice to follow the wide valleys rather than trying to vault the high terrain in a basic airplane. I don't think I got over 9,500 feet, and that was only for a short time while negotiating one of the higher passes. And I remember thinking that you can indeed get a better feel for how our land is arranged by flying across it at low altitude in a light airplane than any other way. I thought about that trip when flying across the mountains at 23,000 feet in my P210 one day. The high trip was supremely comfortable, but the low trip had been a lot more fun.

COMFORT

While my Skyhawk was not a lot faster or more capable than my Pacer, the airplane was a lot more comfortable. The Pacer was a product of the day when you flew wearing an overcoat in the winter and even that wouldn't keep your feet warm. The Hawk had good heat and a lot more room in the cabin. It was progress, even if it did lack the jaunty look of the little Piper. Either airplane worked well when the surface wind was high, although the tailwheel Pacer certainly required a finer touch on the rudder pedals lest it turn around and look at you on the ground.

Basic airplanes are great for basic flying which is, really, whatever you want to do within the performance capability and the limitations of the airplane. The newer ones are more comfortable and the older ones are more fun. There is just as much requirement in a basic for a professional approach to flying because they can and do kill people who don't treat them with the respect that airplanes demand in return for low-risk flying. And a pilot flying a basic has no reason not to be as proud of his airplane and his flying as a Concorde captain. The main thing is to fly; the equipment used is but a variation on the theme.

CUT ABOVE

After basic airplanes come the 140 knotters that add more to traveling ability than a mere 20 knots might suggest. I have owned three of these airplanes—a Skylane, a Cherokee Six, and a Cardinal RG; while the three had entirely different personalities, they all served well. It's funny how you branch out a little more with a faster airplane. I flew my Skylane from New

Jersey to Arizona a couple of times; the Cherokee Six went to Montana and the Cardinal RG went all over the eastern half of the U.S. But in truth the extra climb, speed, and ceiling of the latter two airplanes didn't enable me to do anything that the Skyhawk couldn't do.

In fact, when it comes to dealing with weather in flat, low-elevation country—or even in the mountains—a pilot who would try something in a Skylane that he wouldn't try in a Skyhawk is looking for a lot of trouble. They might be a little better for some things, but not enough to make it possible to tackle meaner hunks of weather. The folks on the ramp might look at you like you are crazy when you arrive on a grungy day in a basic airplane. But the basic ones are easier to manage than the more complicated airplanes and give the pilot extra time to think and to manage the risks that are involved in flying any light airplane in IFR conditions.

The risks in flying any of these singles are remarkably similar and well documented. A lot of them are wrecked because the pilot used up all the fuel, which is easy to avoid. A lot come to grief when the pilot flies them into something—the ground, wires, trees, hills, whatever. There is no way to truly evaluate the specific IFR risks as compared to the VFR risks in the airplanes because no meaningful figures are available, but logic suggests that the exposure to risk is far lower when flying IFR than when flying VFR in marginal conditions. In IFR the primary risks are loss of control, which is both pilot- and equipment-related, and flying into the ground on approach, which is up to the pilot. Some of the secondary risks, less likely but still very much there, are ice, thunderstorms, weather worse than forecast, and mechanical problems.

Except for thunderstorms, which can be rather sudden events, most of the risks in flying 120- to 140-knot

64   airplanes IFR are problems that evolve rather slowly and offer a way out at least once before the event becomes life-threatening. One loss-of-control accident illustrates this. The pilot, flying a single-engine Cessna IFR at night, started having trouble with communication and navigation as the flight progressed. This got continuously worse and the airplane was finally completely out of touch with the controllers. The pilot subsequently lost control and crashed. The alternator charging system on the aircraft had failed. The pilot apparently didn't notice this and flew on until the battery was depleted. There was apparently no flashlight on board so when the lights went out, the lights went out. If, when the alternator first failed, the pilot had turned off all nonessential electrics and made a bee-line for the nearest suitable airport, the flight might have had a happier ending.

A similar risk was managed better by a couple of pilots flying an airplane on which the starter hung, or remained engaged, after the engine was started. Night IFR again. In this condition a starter spins until it burns up and when it does this it is running a lot of current the wrong way through the system, which can and does completely ace the electrical system of the airplane. Trouble is, it will usually give you time to take off before it blows everything. (When a starter is hung, there should be an abnormal reading on the ammeter. Some airplanes have a hung-starter warning light.) It did this evening; the lights and everything else went out after the airplane had entered clouds on an IFR climb. There was a good flashlight in this airplane and the pilot flew it between layers to near his original destination where he descended below the clouds and, when he couldn't find an airport, managed a successful off-airport landing. There is always the risk of something failing; it did

for this pilot and he had the basic equipment (a flash-   65
light) and the cool to manage the emergency.

When you are flying marginal VFR, the risk is almost continuous. When flying IFR, if all the procedures
are followed and the airplane is kept under control, the
risks can be kept in abeyance until something unusual
happens.

HARDWARE HELP

Because of a lot of events over the years there is hard-
ware available to manage many of the risks in relatively simple singles. For thunderstorms there is the
Stormscope, which can be fitted in any airplane, and
radar, which is available for some airplanes. And when
I look at the progress that has been made in the 33 years
that I have been flying IFR, this is the biggie. Having
on-board equipment that tells of rain and/or lightning
makes more difference to me than any other development during this period. I could fly and talk and navigate and make approaches in my Pacer, but I made a lot
of buttonholes in the seat cushion while contemplating
the possibility of imbedded thunderstorms. And I got
beat up in the airplane a few times. The same thing was
true in my Skyhawk, Skylane, and Cherokee Six, and in
the Comanches, Twin Comanches, Twin Bonanza, and
other airplanes that I operated. Then, in 1976, Paul Ryan
called and asked if I wanted to try one of his new
Stormscopes. I have never been without one since, combined in my P210 with radar, and it does make a difference. There is no yes-no window, nor does it make it
possible to fly light airplanes through thunderstorms. It
will show you where lightning is in relation to the nose
of the airplane, and it thus defines the simplest princi-
ple of thunderstorm avoidance: Don't point the nose

66 of the airplane at clouds that are spewing electricity.

The risk of vacuum failure can be addressed with a standby vacuum system or standby instruments. The possibility of nav-com failure can be managed with one of the new handhelds that allow communication as well as VOR navigation. And the faster the airplane becomes, the more important it is to consider every risk and take every possible measure to safeguard against those risks.

The one risk that can't be totally managed is the failure of the engine in any single. This is simply a risk that has to be accepted. Engines don't quit completely very often, as long as they are fed and maintained properly. But the stark fact remains that they can and do fail, and there are more moments in IFR than VFR flying where the complete failure of an engine would serve up substantial risk. This can be minimized by following very conservative en route weather minimums. If there is ceiling beneath, then a power-off landing would offer options after the airplane breaks out of the clouds. Not flying over ridges when they are obscured reduces risk. Not flying at night also reduces risk.

On the other hand, the accident record shows the mechanical failure of an engine while a single is IFR to be an event that is not often serious. It's simply up to the pilot to study all the possibilities and act accordingly. Certainly a pilot who makes a low-visibility takeoff and flies for hours over fog-shrouded countryside in a single is accepting a far higher risk in case of engine failure than does a pilot who waits for the fog to lift before taking off. But by the same token, a pilot who operates a single out of a relatively small airport surrounded by inhospitable terrain accepts more takeoff and initial climb risk than does a pilot who flies out of a larger airport surrounded by wide-open spaces. The

nice thing about all this is the risk that would come if
the engine failed is always obvious, and pilots tend to
do better with risks that are obvious to them than they
do with risks that come from things they think couldn't
happen to them, such as a loss of control.

FASTER SINGLES

If there is a critical point in the life of a pilot, it comes
as he moves up to airplanes that have the capability of
cruising in excess of 150 knots and the range to fly a
third of the way across the country without stopping,
some of which have a very large useful load and some
of which are turbocharged. These airplanes do much
more than their simpler siblings, and the consequences
of a mistake can be far more serious.

Why so critical? Because these faster airplanes are
more demanding of the pilot and less forgiving of any
looseness in operation. This is, at least into late 1987, an
area that is not addressed by regulation or widespread
formal education. As a result, the accident rates in
faster airplanes are worse than in slower ones. It's not
possible to say, for example, that a Skyhawk is twice as
safe as a 210, but I would bet that were numbers available, they would show that pilots wreck these airplanes
at least in proportion to the increase in speed.

The much-maligned and now modified V-tail Bonanza is a good example of what happens when pilots
step up to fast, aerodynamically clean airplanes. While
it has been the airplane selected for ballyhoo and TV
coverage, it actually has an accident record that appears better than the average for this class of airplane.
And when it comes to in-flight structural failures, the
Cessna 210s and Piper PA-32s have similar records to
the V-tail. But there are a lot of V-tails out there, and

68 they have been involved in a corresponding number of airframe failures in flight in the 40 years that they have been in the general aviation fleet.

Airframe failures occur in single-engine retractables far more than in any other class airplane. While other airplanes have about the same rate of fatal accidents after a loss of control, the airframe failure is both spectacular and used by some as an example that there was something wrong with the structure. In reality, all loss-of-control accidents are virtually identical in the way the sequence begins and the final result. The only difference is in the airplane hitting the ground in one piece, or in several pieces. In any airplane, if the pilot loses control and does not regain it quickly, the airplane might well reach a nonsurvivable condition from which no successful recovery is possible. A spiral dive is a condition in which the airplane is in a screaming, twisting plummet that develops quickly when control is lost. And until airplanes are made laterally stable by regulation, with stability augmentation systems, the risk of entering a spiral will be there, waiting for the pilot to miss his cue.

CONFIGURATION

Another factor has to be considered regarding the high incidence of airframe failures in single-engine retractables. The general configuration of these airplanes simply makes them more vulnerable to this phenomenon than other light airplanes. Especially when the quantity of fuel in the wing tanks is low, the weight is concentrated in the center so the bending loads on the wings will be high when G loads are imposed on the airframe. On a twin, the engines and tip tanks (if applicable) tend to help relieve these loads, and as a result the incidence of airframe failures in twins is relatively low. On fixed-gear singles, the drag of the landing gear keeps speed from building as fast. That leaves the sleek retractable right in the middle and the record proves their vulnerability. People can and do lose control of other airplanes with about the same frequency, and the accidents that result are just as disastrous. But the airframe does not fail as often.

The spiral starts with a loss of lateral control. Steep bank, what happens? The nose drops. Steep bank, what happens when you pull back on the elevator control? Nothing good, that's for sure. With the airplane over on its side, pulling back on the wheel only tends to steepen the dive. The speed goes out of sight, the nose is pointed at the ground, the G load is high. Once it fully develops, if the pilot who lost control does the correct thing, roll the wings level, it is doubtful that the recovery can be completed without bad things happening. If the airplane is indicating 150 at cruise, it was trimmed for that speed. In the spiral the airplane accelerates to a speed far in excess of its cruise speed and is going faster than the design dive speed which has to be, by rule, 150 percent of the top of the green arc on the airspeed indicator. This is the maximum speed that is considered in certification and testing. (The redline, which should never be exceeded, is less than the dive speed which, on a 210 for example, would be 247 knots.) Roll the wings level at the estimated 300 knots that some airplanes reach in a spiral dive and the airplane will go for its 150-knot trim speed.

IN THE MIND OF THE PILOT

It's not possible to get inside the mind of a pilot at the beginning of a spiral dive loss of control, but if you

70   could, you would probably find a measure of confusion plus a refusal to immediately acknowledge that the airplane is in trouble. This speculation is supported by the fact that pilots in spiral dives seldom do two things that would help their situation. In most cases, the pilot does not reduce power or extend the landing gear, neither of which is a cure-all, but either of which would serve to lessen the rate of speed increase.

To show how fast an airplane can reach an unrecoverable condition, consider two well-documented losses of control in four-engine turboprop Lockheed Electras. The first loss of control came after electrical problems had disabled some of the flight instruments. To begin, the airspeed of the aircraft was 200 knots (the aircraft was climbing at the beginning of the event) and it remained at or below 240 knots in the first part of the loss of control. Then, in the airplane's last 30 seconds, the heading changed very rapidly, indicating a loss of lateral control, the rate of descent was in excess of 12,000 feet per minute, the airspeed increased to 330 knots, and the G load increased to almost 6 Gs, at which time the airplane broke up in flight. They were in trouble before that last 30 seconds, and then things unravelled quickly.

In another Electra, this one trying to turn around in an area of severe weather, the airspeed increased from about 200 knots to about 360 knots over a period of eight seconds while the heading changed almost 180 degrees in under 20 seconds. When the airplane broke up, it was descending at an estimated 28,800 feet per minute. It can and does happen quickly, and when a pilot discards his trusty old fixed-gear airplane for a flashy retractable, the risks associated with a loss of control increase and can be managed only by matching the new airplane's higher performance with a higher level of training and proficiency.

NO SOLUTION YET

There is no solution as such to the spiral dive phenomenon other than pilot training or stability augmentation. The training is rather like that you give a child about not falling out of a window, or a dog about not jumping out of the back of a pickup truck going 70 miles per hour. It is a matter of learning not to let the airplane wander into a spiral dive because once it is there, in a fully developed spiral, it is not likely that a pilot who allowed the airplane to enter such a maneuver will be able to muster the instant ability to get it out. The recovery would simply be far more difficult and critical than the prevention.

The other solution, a mechanical-electronic one, will only come on demand, and it is hard to tell whether or not we who fly will ever demand that this be done. Many of us are loath to admit that we can't do it with our own mind and hand, even though it can be shown that a lateral stability augmentation system would probably prevent a lot of serious accidents every year.

A lot of insurance companies will not write policies on retractable singles unless the pilot has an instrument rating. This is their way of looking at the overall higher accident rate in this class of airplane, and presumably the thinking is that IFR capability will lessen the incidence of loss of control. It is hard to argue with the logic of this. While many pilots who fly in the west might contend that the instrument rating is useless to them because it is either VFR or so violently IFR that you had best stay on the ground, the training for the rating is useful to anyone. The standards for licensing have remained at a minimum level since the days of the J-3 Cub, and anyone wishing to fly something other than the most basic airplane needs further training. The instrument rating is the only available means for formally

72 upgrading a pilot to a more sophisticated use of the airplane and the air traffic control system. And while it is good to get the rating and do the first instrument flying in a basic airplane, this does serve to prepare a pilot for more complex tasks. The key is in not only getting a thorough checkout in the faster airplane, but also a thorough IFR checkout in that airplane.

One of the fringe benefits of the high-performance singles is the availability of flight control systems, weather-avoidance gear, and anti-icing capability. All this good stuff carries with it a responsibility for training, because in itself it does not enable anything. Equipment only serves the purpose of giving the pilot more information: He has to use it.

STORMS OR NOT?

The most complete information you can get on storms comes from a combination of airborne weather radar and a Stormscope. While this combination is ideal, having the two together, or either one separately, does not mean you can part the waters in a light airplane.

The trip was from New Jersey to Florida. In New Jersey heavy rain was falling and the TV weather folks were calling the heavy rain "thunderstorms." The aviation forecasts did not include the chance of thunderstorms until afternoon, calling only for rainshowers. But it was raining by the bucket. At the airport, the big hangar had endured a flash flood and they were pumping water out of it onto the ramp.

The Stormscope showed no electrical activity in the area, and, using the radar, I could see that the direction in which I was going was devoid of strong cells—at least for the first few miles. The radar map I got before takeoff had shown a little heavy rain and a lot of moder-

ate rain in the area, but this had apparently moved off
to the east. The real activity was in the Carolinas, and
was covered by a convective sigmet for a line of thunderstorms moving toward the south, maximum tops to
45,000 feet.

The ride in rain was fine, and soon the airplane was
on top at 14,000 feet. The activity to the south was
strong enough to put dots on the Stormscope set on the
200-mile range.

The original filed destination was Florence, South
Carolina. The controllers said there was a lot of
weather down that way, and one suggested that the
easterly route would delay entry into the weather area
for as long as possible. I elected to fly as low as possible, so was talking to Fayetteville, N.C., approach control when getting close to the area where decisions
would have to be made. The lad there said they had a
commuter that had taken off at Florence and was trying
to pick his way through, but thus far had done nothing
but make circles. All I was going to do was buy gas so
I thought I'd head for Myrtle Beach. The pattern on the
Stormscope indicated that I might be able to get there;
if not, the path to Wilmington, N.C., northeast of Myrtle,
was clear of electrical activity.

There was talk of moderate turbulence in a 737 on
approach to Myrtle Beach AFB, south of the airport I
would be using. On close examination there was a lot
of moderate rain on the radar, some heavy rain, and a
great deal of activity shown on the Stormscope set on
the shortest range. The only spot that looked good on
the radar had a lot of electrical activity. I went to Wilmington to buy a soda pop and make some phone calls.

About an hour later, after a nasty-looking collection of black clouds moved by Wilmington, I took off
again. The rain and electricity were still there, but this

74 time the bad weather had spread out a bit and it was possible to find a path that was clear of both electricity and anything other than light rain. It took some twisting and turning, and there was an ever-present requirement to have a plan to use in case the weather ahead became solid.

The moral to that story is that having all the gear in the airplane doesn't mean you can fly through hell for love every time. The equipment has to be used to make decisions on whether to keep going or to punt. Wing loading and the basic size of an airplane has a lot to do with how it behaves in convective turbulence. Even the heaviest retractable single is still a light airplane, and all the equipment in the world won't make it into a heavy.

Relate to a Heavy

The last thunderstorm that I rode through was in a 727. I was in the jump seat and watched the crew as they tried to interpret a radar that wasn't working perfectly. But it was plain to see on the radar, and out the windshield, that if we were to go to the destination without flying hundreds of miles out of the way, we would have to tackle some rough stuff. They picked the best-looking spot, both visually and on the radar, set the power and speed for rough running, and flew into the area of weather. The captain was hand flying the airplane, and to say that he was working hard would be an understatement. But as I watched the reaction of the 727 to the gyrations of the cell I could sure see a difference in what it was doing and what a light airplane would have been doing in the same situation. The displacements were less and the rolling moments seemed much more subdued. If anything, it was behaving about like a re-

tractable does in a puffy, building cumulus that tops out   75
at 10,000 feet above the ground. Once on the ground the
captain wrote up the radar, but had it been working
perfectly I doubt if the ride would have been much
smoother. What was a bumpy, sometime lurching ride
in the 727 would have been a pilot's nightmare in a light
airplane.

ICE AVOIDANCE

The deicing or anti-icing equipment that we can buy for
singles has to be treated much the same way as
weather-avoidance gear. It does not enable us to fly
through a lot of ice. What it does is give something to
use if ice is encountered, something to use while fleeing
the icing condition. The FAA goes through the exercise
of approving airplanes for flight in icing conditions
which, to many, is a questionable practice. This implies
that flying the airplane in continuous icing is okay. It
isn't. On many airplanes with boots, so much ice builds
up on unprotected surfaces that a substantial airspeed
loss results, and such unhappy things as engine over-
heating can become a factor as the airplane slows and
the cowling ices over.

   What the icing equipment does is allow a pilot to
have a look. The forecast ice is not always there, but if
you challenge the forecast barefooted, and the ice is
there, then you have been caught trespassing. The
boots, or TKS systems, add some options if the forecast
of icing is correct. Operating my deiced airplane for
eight years and 4,000 hours, not once did I have to cancel a flight because of ice. And I probably didn't have
to use the equipment in anger more than a dozen times.
But if I hadn't had it to use those times, the flights in
question might well have been pretty dicey. And there

76   were a lot of flights that I wouldn't have started or continued without it.

An example of freezing rain came one January day as I approached my home base. The whole flight had been one where you would have stayed on the ground unless you had deicing equipment, but the actual ice that accumulated was light. Closer to home, though, we started hearing horror stories about heavy icing in freezing rain at lower altitudes. A sigmet was issued for heavy icing below 5,000 feet. The surface temperature at home was barely above freezing.

The plan was to stay above 5,000 feet and descend at the last minute—if the controller would allow. The alternate plan was to go back to Baltimore, where the surface temperature was more comfortably above freezing. When I spoke with the approach controller, though, he said that there were a lot of airplanes flying around in the area at all altitudes and nobody was complaining about ice or asking for special handling. And there was little on the approach. But given the reports, it wouldn't have been wise to approach the area without having an alternative to turning into a flying popsicle.

The faster and more aerodynamically clean the aircraft to which it is hooked, the more serious the potential consequences of any misuse of optional equipment, regardless of what the piece of equipment is. And we have to be very careful not to think that radar and Stormscope enable penetration of thunderstorms, that deicing equipment means the aircraft can be flown in continuous icing conditions, or that it is okay to shoot 200 and a half ILS approaches with an autopilot even though the pilot is so rusty he would probably not be able to hand fly the approach.

The next step up from a retractable is a small twin. By definition a light twin is one with a gross weight less than 6,000 pounds. In reality, all the piston twins with under 400 horsepower per side are quite similar in the way they are used and the way they have to be flown, regardless of weight.

A lot of my friends have asked why I don't fly a twin. Well, I used to fly a Twin Bonanza and a Twin Comanche and have some time in all the light twins. And while the airplanes have a lot of positive attributes, the faster singles always seemed like the best deal for what I was doing with an airplane. However, that's strictly a "to each his own" question. If, after a pilot noodles over the attributes of, for example, a Bonanza and a Baron, he feels he will be better off in a Baron, then that would be the proper selection.

What are the plusses for the twin? The obvious ones relate to having two engines instead of one. Two generators and two air pumps for instrument and deice power, plus having the propulsion divided, has to be worth something. In singles, the redundancy of systems can also be answered, which leaves the division of power as the primary difference.

If a twin has a stalling speed of over 61 knots, it must have a minimum rate of climb at 5,000 feet to be certifiable. That, on a twin without turbochargers, adds a very nice low-level asset. If the airplane has enough power to meet the climb requirement at 5,000 feet on one engine, it has a lot of power available for climb at lower altitudes when both engines are operating normally. It also has power for cruise at lower altitudes, and at 6,000 or 7,000 feet an airplane like a Baron or Aerostar can do quite nicely. The high initial rate of

78   climb and the snappy low-level cruise combine with the aura of the airplane to emphasize another attribute: ego satisfaction. Anybody who thinks that ego has no role in airplane selection just doesn't know pilots.

But the primary reason for buying a twin is the ability to continue flight after the failure of an engine —in most circumstances.

Managing the Twins

I was droning along southwestbound, north of Charleston, West Virginia, in a Twin Bonanza when the right engine belched and rumbled and smoke started coming out of the breather atop the engine. The way it was running, and the smoke that was being emitted, led to an unavoidable conclusion: Shut the engine down, go to the nearest airport, and land. The nearest large airport was Charleston; I flew there and made an uneventful landing. The engine had swallowed a valve. It would have run a little longer but not a lot longer, so the decision to shut it down was a good one.

Flying a new Seneca one day, a nonpilot colleague riding in the back seat tapped me on the shoulder with a question. "Does this airplane have the skywriting option?" What prompted the question was a stream of white smoke coming out of the right engine. Whatever was making that much smoke was certainly worthy of consideration and the decision was quickly made to shut the engine down. The oil filter was loose, about to come off, and was allowing engine oil to escape onto the turbocharger, making copious amounts of white smoke.

I've had two other actual shutdowns of engines in twins. How do you explain having had seemingly more engine problems in twins than singles, with about 14 hours in singles to every hour flown in twins? I honestly

do not know the answer to that question. It could be   79
that we are more willing to shut down an engine in a
twin than we are to pull the throttle back in a single and
land immediately when an engine is rough. In my 210,
I had a couple of cases of a failed magneto making the
engine run rough. Had it been a twin, I might indeed
have feathered the engine. In the single it was a matter
of flying to the nearest suitable airport and landing. In
my Skyhawk, when it started running on only three of
four cylinders because of lead fouling, I kept it going,
went to an airport, and landed; in a twin I would probably have shut down an engine that was running like
that.

Having the capability to shut an engine down and
go land is definitely a plus because it is no fun to fly a
rough-running single and the possibility is always there
that a rough-running engine will turn itself into a silent
mass at any time.

The minuses of twins are not so obvious. Anyone
can tell you that a single will come down after the
failure of its engine, while the twin offers the hope of
continued flight. And the hope is only a reality if the
pilot does a virtually perfect job of flying in most twins.
And perfection is something that has historically eluded
many pilots flying light twins with an engine out.

The techniques of flying a twin on one engine are
well taught; perhaps more important is the philosophy
of operating a light twin in a manner that minimizes the
risk of engine failure. This is really where the management of risks unique to this type airplane starts.

I used to fly a Twin Bonanza in and out of a strip
that was 1,500 feet long and have operated a Twin Comanche from an airport of similar size. At such airports,
the whole operation was predicated on both engines
running. If anything happened to one engine, the only

80   thing to do would be shut the other one down and land. So the twin in these cases was really a single, with two chances of engine failure. That was not such a good deal but I recognized it going in and was accepting some additional risk in return for utility. To remove this risk, a twin should be operated only from runways and at weights that would allow a successful continuation or full stop if an engine failed at any point in the proceedings.

A big factor in small twins is loss of control after the failure of an engine. This generally occurs on initial climb after an engine failure, or while maneuvering for landing with one engine shut down. The landing problem might arise if the approach is too low and the pilot attempts to stretch the glide by adding a lot of power at a relatively low airspeed. Or it might come after the pilot overshoots the approach and attempts a go-around on one engine.

Management of the loss-of-control risk because of inadequate airspeed is the same in any airplane. In the twin, the problem is stronger because asymmetric thrust can combine with inadequate airspeed to turn things upside down. But if you stall a Bonanza at low altitude, the end result might be much the same as if you stall a Baron at low altitude. The pilot who is able to precisely control airspeed and who fully understands the hazards of trying to fly too slowly is likely to stay out of this sort of trouble.

In any piston airplane we do have to acknowledge that there is more risk than in, say, a jet. In the single, there is always the chance that the engine might fail, completely and suddenly. Statistically this does not prove to be a big factor in fatal accidents, with few per year identified. But that wouldn't do you a lot of good were you to find yourself flying over fog-shrouded

mountains at night when the crankshaft decided that   **81**
the time to break had come. The chances of this happening are small, but they do exist.

In a twin in that situation, if one engine failed you
could likely fly on to an area where an approach would
be possible. But an engine-out instrument approach requires a high degree of skill, and as the airplane de-
scends, the options lessen and the risk increases. Too,
if the twin is involved in an off-airport landing, the risk
is higher because the touchdown speed will be faster,
and while on the single the heavy part (the engine)
leads the way, on the twin the heavy parts (the engines)
drag the light part (the fuselage) through the rough. On
Transport Category jets there is an answer to every
"what if" question and the answer is almost never
"crash." If we pay less and fly airplanes that are not
certified and operated like Transport Category airplanes, then there are a few questions to which the only
answer is "crash."

TURBINES

Turbine-powered airplanes are the ultimate, and
though the training and proficiency requirements for
most are far in excess of what is required for piston
airplanes, they are really easier to fly. There is a strong
myth associated with this, too. While much is made of
the amount of "turbine time" a pilot might have, there
are a lot of things that a pilot might have that are more
important than what kind of engines he has been herd-
ing around. There is no way to quantify it in terms of
hours or any other measure, but a pilot's ability to think
and properly follow procedures is as important as any
number in a logbook.

One of the reasons the turbines are easier to fly is

82   that the training to fly them is better and more logical than that for light airplanes. In turbines there is universal recognition that there is only one way to fly these airplanes. They are flown precisely, by the numbers. No seat-of-the-pants business. This directly relates to the business about thinking under pressure. With all procedures and techniques taught, the thinking process can address other factors that are working on the flight.

There is something here to learn if light airplanes are the most frequent steed. They respond just as well to precise, procedural flying as do jets. I watched the other day as a pilot totally fouled up an approach to an unfamiliar airport. As we discussed it later, I asked why he didn't make a solid plan for the approach, continually evaluating the number of flying miles left to the end of the runway, the altitude remaining to be lost, the airspeed, and the terrain. His reply was that he just "eyeballs" approaches. That's a loose way to do it, and awkward arrivals can result. This pilot is a product of the light-airplane training system; when the time comes for him to be exposed to advanced training, he'll learn how much easier it is if done by the book, by the numbers, precisely, as in jets.

JET FLIGHT

Ride along on a flight in a jet to see how relatively easy it is to fly.

On this particular airplane there is some nose-wheel steering available through the rudder pedals, while on some other jets a small steering wheel, or tiller, is operated by the captain's left hand to steer in the early stages of the takeoff run. The steering on this one is precise, and tracking the runway centerline is quite easy. If the jet being flown is a larger one, as this one is, then eye height above the runway will be great and the look of acceleration will be slow, but the feel of it will be great because this jet is a powerful one. The final power setting is up to the first officer or flight engineer, if there is one. The first officer calls off the appropriate speeds as the airplane accelerates.

An important call is V1, the speed above which the takeoff would be continued even after the failure of one engine. This speed comes before Vr, the speed at which you lift off. If there had been trouble before reaching V1, the airplane could be stopped on the remaining runway.

On this takeoff V1 is 160 knots and Vr 199. When the pilot in the right seat calls "rotate," the nose is brought smoothly to 14 degrees nose-up. As the attitude approaches the desired value, a little of the back pressure used to bring the nose up is relaxed so as not to overshoot the target attitude. As the airplane accelerates and approaches the 250 knots that is a speed limit below 10,000 feet, another nose-up pitch adjustment is required—in this case to 19 degrees nose-up.

Flying around level at a maneuvering altitude, the airplane is much the same as any other, and the power is actually easier to manage and less critical to large changes. Honk back on the throttle of a piston engine and it might protest, to say nothing of the damage that shock cooling might do. It takes a lot of power to make jets go fast, and when you remove that power they do indeed slow down and come down. This particular airplane has no speed brakes, as many do, but if there is need for a very rapid descent, reverse can be selected on the two inboard engines.

The approach is flown 10.5 degrees nose-up with the autothrottle system set to maintain 162 knots indicated airspeed. The airplane is very stable in the approach configuration, and with its high wing loading,

84   the little vagaries in the atmosphere don't move it around a lot. When the mains are 15 feet above the ground, per the flight engineer's altitude callouts, the power is retarded and a slight amount of nose-up combines with ground effect to make the touchdown smooth. The key was a stabilized approach. Get it there at the precise airspeed, and with the sink rate right on, and every landing will be the same. Once on, the nosewheel is lowered to the runway and reverse is selected. The flight engineer calls 100 knots on the deceleration, and the airplane appears to be going very slowly at that speed due to eye height above the runway.

That's a flight in the ultimate jet, Concorde, which, once it is learned, works about like any other airplane. Do your best to fly a perfect flight and the reward is there.

It has always been bothersome that the accident rate in light airplanes is so much worse than it is in turbine-powered airplanes. And, in turbines, it is bothersome that the accident rate in turboprops is higher than it is in jets. The airplanes have something to do with this because the pure jet probably sets the standard for reliability, and the regulations require that they be operated in a manner that ensures success even if an engine fails at the worst possible time.

But the larger factor is the way pilots prepare for flying the airplanes, and the way they are operated. No kidding, if you are flying a jet you have to understand the systems and procedures to get the type rating, and you have to fly the airplane precisely and per the book to get the type rating. And everyone who flies a jet understands that this is no seat-of-the-pants operation. There is something there for all of us to learn even when flying slower airplanes. The seat-of-the-pants business ended with biplanes and Cubs.

LONG DAY

One of the most enjoyable days of flying I have ever had combined two airplanes that I very much like to fly. Far apart in capability, a Cessna P210 and a Lear 35 were flown this day, starting early in the morning in Wichita, Kansas. The first hop was in the Learjet, to Tucson, Arizona. That took only an hour and 50 minutes and because we left early, and there is a time difference, it was still early when we got to Tucson.

The next thing on the menu was to fly my P210 back to New Jersey from Tucson. My son was along, and at the time he had a private license and instrument rating plus quite a lot of flying in the Cessna. So I had good help for the long day.

It was almost noon on the east coast when we left Tucson. The weather was fine, but there was no tail-wind this day and the flight across the desert and plains to Oklahoma City was uneventful, if a little bit slow. The temperature on the ground at Oke City was 96, so we didn't linger long there before launching for Louisville, Kentucky.

The weather on this leg wasn't as good. The haze of summer was prevalent but it was still okay. The airplane was performing perfectly and, in total, it was a nice ride.

It was almost nine in the evening when we left Louisville. I had had a couple of good naps along the way so felt rested, but as we started to leave Louisville I could see the effects of the long day starting to take a toll on my partner, who was in the left seat. A jet was departing on the cross runway to ours and was airborne going through the intersection. I asked Richard what the considerations of wake turbulence would be for our departure and while he answered quickly, he answered

86   backward when he knew better. That was a reminder that long days like this are a bad idea unless there are two pilots along for checks and doublechecks, and so each can have naptime.

Launching into the early evening haze had a special feel to it, and we were soon above the haze and cruising in clear sky. There was actually a headwind on this leg and it was about midnight when we landed at Trenton, N.J., and rolled the airplane into the hangar. I drove home thinking how useful airplanes can be.

SUMMER OF '87

As big a day as that one was, it covered only a bit over 2,800 nautical miles. And it took all day. For an illustration of the contrast in airplanes (and time zones), I'll tell you about a flight in the summer of 1987.

I was in London on business with British Airways. Thursday afternoon was spent touring their maintenance base at Heathrow where one Concorde was in for a major hour check. Peering into all the nooks and crannies of the machine was extremely interesting. I could only marvel that they brought the airplane off with the empty weight under 200,000 pounds and, to this point, had seen very little in the way of structural wear, even though the airplane had flown well over 10,000 hours.

My flight home was scheduled out at 7:30 in the evening and it was to be a special ride because my friend Captain John Cook was to be in command. This was my ninth Concorde ride and while I had flown Concorde's simulator with John, I had never flown in the airplane with him. The airplane for the trip was G-BOAG, Alpha Golf, the one that thrilled huge crowds at Oshkosh in 1985 and the lowest-time Concorde in the British Airways fleet.

As they were running the preflight checks they
found that the number three inertial navigation system
was inoperative. It had to be changed before we could
leave, and as a result we were twenty-five minutes past
the scheduled departure time before pushing back from
the terminal.

The jumpseat in Concorde is right behind the captain and the view of the action is quite good. As we
were cleared into position for takeoff, an Airbus was
cleared to go from an intersection ahead of us. And you
know what? Concorde pilots think about the same thing
that 210 pilots think about. In the late evening haze of
London summer, John watched the Airbus lift off and
climb steeply and said, "Let's not be in any rush to go
and fly in that air he stirred up." So we hesitated before
John gave the order to go. Even then you could feel the
disturbance from the Airbus as Concorde lifted majesti-
cally from the runway and headed out.

Concorde is a complex airplane, but the British
crews know how to operate it, and our trip across the
Atlantic at Mach 2, flying as high as 56,600 feet, was
routine. We'd be a little late getting into Kennedy because you can't make up time in this airplane. It has one
speed, full speed. It is designed to cruise at Mach 2 and
that is where it achieves its best range.

Concorde trips always seem to me to end right after
they start. Traveling across the Atlantic should be a
long journey, but in this airplane it's about like hopping
from Trenton to Indianapolis in my airplane.

They had discussed the approach to Kennedy
along the way. It was to be the notorious Canarsie approach where you come over the Canarsie VOR and
then follow a series of lights in a circle to land on Runway 13 Left. It isn't a popular approach among airline
crews, and it's probably harder to fly in Concorde than
in a slower jet. But John made the arc with grace, rolled

88 the wings level on short final, and made a perfect landing. Every approach I have watched from the jumpseat of Concorde looks grossly high—I always wonder if we are going to land on this airport or the next one—but that's just the nature of the airplane. Runways look short from those high perches, too.

CONCORDE TO BONANZA

The Belt Parkway in New York is notorious for traffic so I had arranged for my FBO, Ronson Aviation, to send a Bonanza to Kennedy. It was there waiting on the British Airways ramp, and I bade Captain Cook goodby beside the Bonanza and headed off home. I walked through the door of my house just before eight in the evening after leaving London just before eight in the evening. Same evening, too. I was actually home in Jersey before Concorde's crew made it to their New York hotel. Bonanzas are neat in their own way.

There is a marvelous contrast in airplanes. They are all good and they all go fast in relation to something. Even a Cub is fast—when compared with a bike. Still, I used to always ride along in my 210 and think how much faster I could get there in a turboprop, or in a jet. But I quit doing that when I made peace with the fact that speed is relative and there is only one really fast airplane, Concorde. The rest of us are just left to fly as fast as we can.

4

The
Challenges

THE CHALLENGES of flying are perhaps the most fun part of the activity. They are both numerous and varied; recognizing and meeting them is a big part of managing the risks of flying.

Maybe flying is not considered to be an elitist activity. But we do have to be realistic and say that not everyone is suited to flying, and a lot of us are not suited for all types of flying. Yet there is no formal weeding out process to help us understand what our adaptability might be for flying. We are basically left on our own, albeit with a rather loose licensing system, to establish some qualification for the various types of flying.

A program undertaken by British Airways shed some light on this subject for me. They started a flying training scheme in 1987 for young people, to ensure an adequate pilot force for the future. The classes were to train 128 pilots a year; for the first class they had 8,800

90   applicants. Now how, pray tell, do you find the best 128 out of 8,800 bright young folks? Their methodology establishes a framework for thought about adaptability for flying.

The initial screening was a written test that was sent to all who expressed interest. This was general in scope and the answers were used to reduce the size of the group to 2,000. Scientifically designed and based on sample tests given to active pilots, this probed the applicant's interests. British Airways is satisfied with the folks who fly for them now so it was logical that the test should be based on things their pilots are interested in and should be a general test on which their current employees do well. For example, did you build model airplanes when you were a kid? That might be construed to show an abiding interest in airplanes from an early age. And they wanted to identify people who are interested in flying and airplanes, not just in the lifestyle of a pilot.

Further tests for the 2,000 who jump the first hurdle take two forms. There is a computerized test that looks at coordination and recognition, and there is personality testing.

The coordination-recognition testing was interesting to me because only 46 percent of the people who take it pass. A successful grade is 116 or better (out of a possible 180), and over half the 18- to 23-year-olds who take it don't pass. That means they don't possess the minimum level of coordination that British Airways (and the RAF, with whom they share the test) feel is necessary to fly well. Challenge: A person who couldn't pass this test would find much more challenge in some types of flying, probably aerobatics and instrument flying, than someone who does well on the test.

To devise the personal specifications that are

found in good pilots, British Airways again surveyed
their pilots. Team and analytical skills were found to be
very important, along with the ability to prioritize activities. Short-term memory was found to be more important to flying than long-term memory, though you
have to have some of the latter. (After all, with only
short-term memory you might know present position to
the foot, but might have forgotten the point of departure
and the destination!) Flexibility was found to be a pilot
virtue along with emotional stability, basic technical
knowledge, and general intelligence. Bad traits were
found to be unconventional or unusual values and ad-
venturesomeness. People who take risks for the fun of
it were deemed not to be good pilots, along with those
who are impulsive. The best quick description of a good
pilot? A stable extrovert fills the bill.

Of course, all pilots are not perfect. The challenge
is in identifying any trait that might be considered risky
if taken into the cockpit. Risks can be managed if they
are recognized. For example, the fact that a pilot is a
totally unconventional person when off duty does not
mean that he can't shape up when with airplanes. It's
probably the risk-taking trait that would be the hardest
to manage. A tendency to race the train at a grade
crossing might come to the surface on a nonprecision
approach where a pilot ducks below minimums.

Take what the British think makes a good pilot and
go flying. A self-analysis of all flight operations makes
a fine challenge.

PLANNED FLIGHT

This was a relatively simple flight, from Trenton, New
Jersey, to Punxsutawney, Pennsylvania. The weather
was relatively good with some visibility obscuration at

92 Trenton in fog and cloud cover over the mountains west of Harrisburg, Pennsylvania. A cold front was a few hundred miles west of the route, so the flight would be flown with an increasing headwind.

The first test, perhaps of impulsiveness, came when I learned that there would be a delay in getting an IFR clearance. Another airplane was about to leave on a Special VFR, and as I waited the tower announced that the visibility was now three miles. Go VFR? Even though it is my policy not to do this, I thought about it for a moment. Then I realized, among other things, that I had checked weather for an IFR flight, and what could be an easy IFR might be a hard VFR flight. So I put this thought out of my mind.

Looking back on the flight, I can recognize the requirement to be able to prioritize activities. En route, navigation is important, but so is planning for the arrival. I was not familiar with the area or the airport, so the approach plate had to be studied. The minimum en route and safe altitudes shown on the charts were important numbers to consider. So was the arrival procedure. The runway at Punxsutawney is 3,000 feet long, which means you don't charge in without a plan. Another part of the en route activity was reviewing the procedure for landing on a less-than-long runway. As it turned out, the active runway was also downhill, which made the planning even more important. This consideration of the arrival might be likened to the Concorde crew's discussion of the Canarsie approach. Only I was talking to myself.

The airplane was beneath the clouds 10 or more miles out, and the airport was sighted early. This gave the opportunity to get down to pattern altitude and properly slowed before turning on a one-mile final. The landing was pretty good, and short enough that only about half the runway was used. So the flight was fine, **93** the result coming not from any particular amount of superb airmanship, but simply from meeting the challenge by making plans and then following those plans in a methodical manner.

ROCKY MOUNTAIN HIGH

Another day I was also flying in unfamiliar territory and faced some interesting weather challenges. The run was from San Jose, California, to Montrose, Colorado, where the weather was forecast to be reasonable, but with the chance of a shower or thundershower. And there were flight precautions for mountain obscuration in Colorado and moderate turbulence below 16,000 feet. The early morning radar report showed some activity with tops to 20,000 in southern Colorado, but radar reports don't age well and it would be midday before we reached the area. Because the lowest ceiling forecast for Montrose was 5,000 feet, even in the possible showers, and no mention was made in the forecast of visibility restrictions, no alternate airport was filed. Four hours en route, five plus 15 on the fuel. All tidy and legal.

Flying east out of San Jose, at Flight Level 210, we got a change in plan early. There was an in-flight refuelling ahead and we either had to climb or descend. We climbed to Flight Level 230 where the cabin altitude of my P210 was at almost 12,500 feet. I don't really like that, but there were two of us in the airplane, the other guy was younger than I, and I had recently been in the altitude chamber so was current on the symptoms of hypoxia. (Heard some new terminology on this leg, too. The controller wanted to know the identification of the military airplane being refuelled and he asked

94   the tanker pilot, "Who are you holding hands with?")

There were some big buildups ahead as we neared Montrose. Tops were well above our level. They didn't show much on radar, but then mountain showers and thundershowers often don't make a strong radar return. There isn't a lot of moisture in them. Even though it was May, the temperature aloft was relatively cool, so most of the moisture in the buildups would be snow, which doesn't show all that well on radar. But the Stormscope was showing electrical activity, which meant stay out.

Now, bright guy who didn't consider an alternate because it was not required by law, what will you do if Montrose has a thundershower in progress when you get there? An hour out I decided the decision not to file an alternate was a bad one, and scurried to the chart to look for things we might do if Montrose looked like a bad deal. There were places to go and while I was pleased with the decision to work this problem an hour out instead of a few minutes out, the challenge of flight planning had been poorly met when the "chance of thundershowers" did not prompt some consideration of an alternate.

It almost came true, too. If we had had to fly the complete VOR approach at Montrose, we would have penetrated a big shower that was northwest of the field. As it was, we broke out of clouds right over the airport and were able to make a visual approach.

Leaving Montrose I watched my companion pilot who was flying go through a moment of total confusion. There is a takeoff and departure procedure there because it is in the Rockies. The drill is to climb to 12,400 feet in the holding pattern at the vortac before striking out on course. The holding pattern is northwest of the vortac. After takeoff, I sat wondering what the pilot was doing; he sure as hell wasn't entering a holding pattern northwest of the station in any manner that I had ever

seen. A discussion ensued and I finally told him, in no   95
uncertain terms, to make a left turn back around to the
vortac. He did, and by the time we got there we had
reached the requisite altitude and could fly on eastbound down the airway. What caused the problem? He
had glanced at the chart and thought the pattern was on
the southeast leg. He just had his directions reversed.
We had a void time on the clearance, and it had taken
an extra couple of minutes to get the engine going. So,
hurry. But don't hurry so much that you don't take the
time to doublecheck everything.

Something else could have been a factor, and I
have to admit that I didn't think about it until writing
this. We had just spent the better part of four hours at
a cabin altitude of 12,500 feet, and while on the ground
the elevation was almost 6,000 feet. That can dull the
old brain and any time you aren't thinking at 100-per-
cent power, you need to cut yourself some extra slack.
This primarily means you have to doublecheck everything.

IMPULSIVENESS VERSUS DECISIVENESS

If being impulsive is not good, but a pilot has to be
decisive, how do we separate the two? One example to
consider might be that of the airline crew that wound up
60 miles off course over the Atlantic and almost collided
with another airliner. Much was made in the news of
the crew allegedly asking the other crew not to report
the incident. That might be called an impulsive reaction, and rare is the person who hasn't said something
that he later regretted. If after discovering the error, the
crew had put all its effort into getting the aircraft back
on course, then you might say that the initial error was
followed by a good decision.

Sometimes when we are flying we might do things

96   that we later regret, and, presuming that we survive such an event, the later analysis of it can be a valuable challenge in honing our relationship to aviation.

Probably the most frequent impulsive behavior relates to the radio, where some of us are prone to grab the mike and drop the ball. If the clearance or instruction from an air traffic controller isn't what is wanted, some argue, grouse, question, or pout. A decisive pilot, though, will do none of those things. Being decisive means following the clearance quickly and to the letter. If there is some argument, it can and should be handled on the phone after landing. I know the times I have had words with controllers on the radio I have always looked back and regretted that I couldn't control my displeasure with the clearance.

More dangerous impulsive behavior relates both to flying technique and to decisions to do things with the airplane that are hazardous.

DECISION TIME

According to the National Transportation Safety Board report, the pilot who was ferrying a Cessna P210 across the Atlantic was "anxious to go." The leg ahead was from Goose Bay, Labrador, to Narssarssuaq in Greenland with an alternate airport of Nuuk, Greenland. The weather at the proposed destination was forecast to be 1,000 scattered, 3,500 overcast, visibility 10 kilometers or better with temporary conditions of 800 obscured, visibility 1,500 meters in rain and snow. Surface winds were to be southwesterly and gusty. The forecast for Nuuk was worse. A VFR flight plan was authorized by Transport Canada for flight at or below 5,500 feet from Goose Bay to Narssarssuaq and the pilot filed with an estimated time en route of five hours and a fuel endur-

ance of seven hours. The aircraft had standard 89-gal-
lon tanks; for seven hours' endurance the engine would
have to be run at about 50-percent power.

As the pilot proceeded toward Narssarssuaq, he
checked weather and the news was not good. Precip
was falling, and the wind was out of the east much
stronger than forecast, with peak gusts to 38 knots.
Nuuk, the alternate, was reporting freezing rain and
strong winds.

Narssarssuaq is surrounded by mountainous terrain and the approach from the west is through fjords.
For a daytime VFR approach, pilots without a good
knowledge of local conditions are advised not to attempt a VFR approach to the airport unless the ceiling
is at least 4,000 feet and the flight visibility is at least
five miles. There are three instrument approaches, all
with relatively high minimums, and the approach chart
cautions that the approach should not be attempted if
winds exceed 30 knots. Reported visibility was below
minimums for either a VFR or an IFR approach to the
airport. The visibility at the alternate was adequate for
the approach but the reported ceiling was below the
minimum descent altitude.

The pilot notified the flight information center that
he intended to divert to Reykjavik, Iceland. He estimated arrival there at 1717 with an estimated time of
fuel exhaustion of 1846. It was January over the North
Atlantic, which is a bad time and place to be running
tanks down low.

At about 1712 the aircraft was identified on radar
by Iceland's air traffic control center. It was 188 miles
west of Keflavik; two minutes later the pilot reported
that the aircraft was low on fuel. Two minutes after that
he reported that one hour of fuel remained. Because of
a report of more favorable winds higher, the pilot initi-

98   ated a climb from 5,500 to 15,000 feet. Even though the pilot had not declared an emergency, the authorities initiated search and rescue activities with USAF aircraft and Icelandic ships sent toward the Cessna. A weather summary reported that surface winds over the sea would be between 28 and 40 knots with ocean swells between five and seven meters. There was an overcast at 900 feet with good visibility beneath.

At about 1811, 6.4 hours after takeoff, the fuel was gone. The pilot of a USAF C-130 gave ditching instructions to the pilot and, because it was dusk, the C-130 launched flares to light up the sea. The airplane was ditched, and three minutes later a rescue helicopter arrived. While the airplane was still visible, there was no sign of the occupants. Rescuers lost sight of the airplane about eight minutes after it was ditched. The emergency locator transmitter operated for about 15 minutes after the ditching. Neither the airplane nor the occupants were recovered.

This pilot made a lot of decisions. Would you have launched across the North Atlantic in January with forecasts like those given to this pilot? Just for the sake of exploration, let's say yes. This pilot had flown the route before, so he had some familiarity with it. Did he have doubts about whether or not it would work? There is no way to know that, but from reading the report it is apparent that there were not a lot of margins. At the time the pilot received the Narssarssuaq weather that was below minimums, there were not a lot of courses of action that would have led to success. If the pilot had elected to return to Goose Bay, the board calculated that it might not have made it back to the airport, but that it could have reached the Labrador coast if flown efficiently. The airplane should have been able to reach the alternate, Nuuk, but the weather there was no prize.

The climb to 15,000 feet was deemed to have had no
effect on where the airplane ditched. If the whole flight
had been flown at 10,000 feet it might have made Iceland but the margin for error would have been extremely small.

When studying accidents you can see a lot of the
things covered in the British Airways testing at play.
The impulsive (which means actuated or swayed by
emotional or involuntary impulses) launching or continuing of flights in bad weather is the cause of many
accidents, especially involving pilots trying to fly VFR
when it isn't. Managing this, and sorting out the difference between doing something impulsive and making
good decisions, is a key to flying.

MECHANICAL VERSUS MENTAL CHALLENGES

This pilot had no trouble with the mechanics of flying.
The airplane was under control until it hit the water,
and had the waves not been so big he might have made
a gentle enough arrival to have gotten out and it might
have had a happy ending. Too often we judge pilots by
the mechanical abilities and rote knowledge of the rules
rather than by the ability to think accurately and rapidly and to make the right decisions.

CONFIDENCE

Having confidence in one's ability is an asset in flying,
as long as it does not grow into overconfidence. And
confidence can ebb and flow in the wrong direction if
it is not properly managed.

I could tell at dinner that the private pilot had a tale
to tell. When he finally got to the story, it was a good
example of how a relatively inexperienced pilot can run

100   the gauntlet of confidence and lack thereof in a relatively short period of time.

The flight was at night, behind a slow-moving cold front that spawned a lot of thunderstorms. The briefer told the pilot that the weather to the south, along the route, would clear as the front moved on to the east.

The flight went well as the pilot and his passenger droned through the night sky. Then the tone changed a little. An approach control facility told the pilot that he would be unable to hand him off to the next facility because they had a power outage due to storms an hour or so earlier. So our pilot was suddenly on his own. Then he learned the old lesson about not being able to see clouds coming at night. The little airplane was suddenly engulfed in clouds. The pilot had always been told to turn around and fly back to where you came from in case of an inadvertent entry into clouds, and so he immediately started to turn. The aircraft was soon in a 60-degree or steeper bank, the vertical speed was down and increasing, the altimeter was unwinding rapidly, and the airspeed was building. The pilot said he thought that his time might have come—his confidence was gone—but the passenger started telling him that he could do it, that he could right the airplane. The soothing voice helped and the pilot soon had the airplane back under control.

The next thing that happened to him was a feeling of being lost. Even though he had known where he was a few moments earlier, the cloud entry and near loss of control had erased from his mind any idea about position. He finally made contact with a radar controller who vectored him to a large airport where he landed, shaken but okay.

There were some notable lessons for him in this. To begin, when the airplane entered the clouds, the autopilot was on. He turned the autopilot off and attempted to turn the airplane around. The autopilot didn't know whether or not the airplane was in clouds, and could have continued maintaining control of the airplane if the pilot had left it alone. A factor that was favorable for the pilot was the fact that the airplane was a fixed-gear single. Had it been a slick retractable, the pilot likely would not have lived to tell the story.

The biggest lesson this pilot learned was that you can't see clouds at night, and that if night VFR cross-country is to be attempted at all, it should be limited to severe clear weather, preferably with a moon. This pilot went to work on an instrument rating after this little episode, which is the smart thing to do if you want to fly at night.

After he finished relating the tale he asked two of us, both pilots with a lot more experience than he had, how many scary moments like that we had had in flying. I had trouble thinking of any because one of the greatest challenges in flying is to not do anything you don't know how to do, and to avoid anxious moments. The world is full of roller-coasters for thrills; I like my airplane flying to be routine and without thrills.

For most pilots, scary times happen close to the beginning of a flying career. And even when they happen there, it has to be charged to not meeting the challenge to learn to do things well, taking it slowly and methodically to build the ability to fly from here to there on a reasonable schedule. As pilots we like to tell war stories; if the war stories are true then there is a chink in the armor. It's a combination of our attitude toward flying and the training process which has been woefully lacking in many areas. In the British Airways selection program they viewed as a liability the willingness to take risks for fun. That is something we need to think

102 about when flying. If, for example, you pull a buzz job for thrills, that is a bad sign. A pilot who does so is likely to be dangerous in every area.

MEET THE CHALLENGE

Flights have all manner of differences in the level of difficulty, and it is up to us to prepare for and meet each level. You can tell a little in advance about how difficult a flight is going to be, but you have to always be prepared for the unexpected.

On a flight from Wichita, Kansas, back to New Jersey the weather was good all the way. The strongest challenges of this flight were on takeoff and landing, and they were routine. No crosswind, good weather, it was really a piece of cake. En route I had only to speak to the controllers when spoken to, maintain altitude, navigate, look for other traffic, and manage the operation of the powerplant. It was a low-challenge trip and the primary thing that could have shattered the reverie would have been a mechanical problem. I reminded myself of that as I flew along and played with the "nearest airport" feature on the Northstar Loran. Every time I checked it at cruise (Flight Level 190), I was within gliding distance of a nice long paved runway. While a power-off landing would have been a challenge, it would have not been that difficult.

I thought back to a trip a couple of years earlier, when the challenges had been stronger.

The goal this day was to meet colleague Mac McClellan, who was coming east in a Cheyenne 400 that he was evaluating. The flight was delayed because of a mechanical problem, and they wound up leaving Oklahoma for New Jersey well after midnight. The Cheyenne had an airborne phone and McClellan called me at about six in the morning with word of another problem. Weather. It was 100 overcast and an eighth of a mile visibility all over the area. We had to have a new plan, and the decision was to land the Cheyenne at Baltimore, which had and was forecast to keep minimums. I would fly to Baltimore to pick up McClellan.

The first challenge was a low-visibility takeoff. This involves an additional element of risk and I thought about that before going. If the engine were to fail it would be a matter of establishing a normal glide and accepting what showed up for a landing. The preflight was extra careful with a doublecheck of anything that could create a demand to return and land, which wouldn't be possible because the weather was below landing minimums. Oil cap tight, fuel caps secure, baggage door secure—things you check for every flight but that I doublecheck for a low-visibility takeoff. More engine problems and aborted takeoffs are caused by pilot action, inaction, or inattention than by anything else. I was determined to manage this part of the risk.

The next step was to psych myself up for the departure. While we used to practice zero-zero instrument takeoffs, I don't think that I would do one for real now. I want enough visibility to track the centerline and had that this morning. But the procedure for a low-visibility takeoff is much the same as for an instrument takeoff. Track the centerline, accelerate to normal rotation speed plus five knots, with the extra speed used to avoid any possibility of touching back. At that speed, transition to the instruments and rotate to 10 degrees nose-up. The primary chore then is to maintain attitude, wings level, cross-checking the standby horizon and the turn coordinator to make certain all are in agreement. Positive rate of climb, gear up. Ninety-five knots, flaps up. Speed at 110, power back to cruise climb. All just

104   like on a clear day, but there is some heightened awareness that it has to be done precisely after a low-visibility takeoff. Once the airplane is configured for cruise
climb, then it's okay to start thinking about something
other than keeping the wings level and flying straight
ahead. In this case, it was a turn on course.

The en route segment to Baltimore was routine instrument flying with no particular demands. But because it was a short flight, I had to start preparing for
the arrival at Baltimore soon after takeoff. I listened to
the ATIS: it would be an ILS to Runway 28, 400 obscured and a mile visibility. On the way in I reminded
myself that in such a situation the weather in the approach area can be worse and that such an approach
has to be treated as one to minimums. I doublechecked
the decision height and gave myself the little lecture
about trying hard to make this one a perfect approach.
It was not misplaced: I was very close to the decision
height when I saw the runway.

The next hop after this was to a small airport in
Ohio, served only by an NDB approach. On this one I
did a poor job of thinking through the approach before
starting in. It was going to have to be a circling approach and instead of slowing the airplane to a good
maneuvering speed, I came in fast and clean. So when
the runway was in sight I had a lot of things to do. Slow
down, get the gear and flaps down, keep the runway in
sight, and judge the approach slope. The approach was
on the high and fast side and the brakes got a good
workout on the stop. I didn't feel that I had done a very
good job of managing that flight.

The next ride was to Toledo, where there is an ILS.
Even though the weather there was relatively good,
with a ceiling of 1,500 feet and a mile visibility, I got the
lecture in order for the arrival, and treated it like an

approach to minimums. The last leg for the day was back to base, where the weather had improved. And it was on this leg that I got a reminder that there are challenges even to flying in good weather. In the Philadelphia area an airline crewmember called in, excited, and reported that they had just missed a Cessna 150 by 200 feet. Watching out for other traffic is a challenge that few of us take as seriously as we should.

I made another note on the flight log for this trip. I have always kept up with the number of times that I have shared the same frequency with Air Force One. This was the first time I heard that call sign as they went out and returned—twice in one day. I heard it on the way to Ohio from Baltimore and on the leg from Toledo back to New Jersey. The airplane was flying at FL240 on the way out and FL230 on the return, which would keep the Commander in Chief in a sea-level cabin all the time. But even though he is the boss, they fly in the system just like we do. In fact, on one flight the airplane had to stay at FL230 a little longer than the crew liked—until they passed over my airplane at FL210. I would have moved if I could have; as it was the controller handled the two flights with equal justice for all.

THE GREATEST CHALLENGE

There is one challenge that adds the most possible excellence to each and every flight and minimizes risk to the maximum extent possible: that one is trying to make every flight the perfect flight. We seldom succeed at this, but it is sure worth trying. Knowing at the end of a flight that you have done your best is satisfying, and if your best is found lacking in some areas, that clearly defines where work is needed on technique or procedures.

106   Some of the folks I work with have at times seemed to smart at this. Gordon Baxter once wrote an article for *Flying* (which we didn't use) entitled "Don't Fly With Collins." That's because I like to have whoever is flying my airplane try for a perfect flight, and I like to carefully examine every glitch, even the slightest. It is interesting to do, and to me it illustrates how a lot of pilots don't receive proper training. It is often obvious that a pilot's instructor never went to the trouble to demand as much perfection as possible. Somehow accepting minimum standards just doesn't work in airplanes.

Simple things mean a lot. Flying a heading is a simple thing, and the good that comes from flying a heading precisely amounts to a lot. I was riding along watching another pilot fly and wondered what he was thinking as he turned back and forth, 30 degrees either side of a correct heading, at the slightest wiggle of the VOR needle. The wind aloft was light so at most a five-degree change would have handled anything. And I wondered if, with virtually everyone learning to fly in fully instrumented airplanes, we aren't losing some of the basics of flying.

SHORT PADDLE

Back in the good old days I used two airplanes for cross-country flying that didn't have a full deck of instruments. One was a Piper PA-12 Super Cruiser; the other was a Swift. Also, I had learned to fly and done all my cross-country training in airplanes without a full gyro panel. Flying with just a compass was harder work than flying with a directional gyro, but it sure taught the value of keeping the wings level. Level wings and the ball in the middle means the heading does not change. So get it right and keep it right.

At the time I had these airplanes I was working in
a civilian contract school that trained pilots for the Air
Force. As always seems the case, my job was in one
place (Georgia) and my heart in another (Arkansas).
But that is what airplanes are for, to span distances, and
I put both the Cruiser and the Swift to good use.

With either, I could leave Georgia after work on
Friday and fly to Arkansas. But I couldn't do it all in
daylight. It would get dark along the way and I learned
more about keeping the wings level on these dark nights
than anywhere else.

A combination of good weather, visual sightings,
the compass, and the turn and bank were the keys to
success on these flights. I would not attempt them unless every station along the way was reporting clear
sky; still, it took a lot of attention to the instrument
panel to keep the airplane on course. I didn't have a
navigational radio either, which meant paying constant
attention to the basics. If I got lost, which I honestly
never did, I would have had to find myself using those
same basic tools and that would be a lot harder than not
getting lost.

I got fooled one night. Even though every station
was reporting clear with at least five miles visibility, it
was quite a distance between stations, between Montgomery, Alabama, and Meridian, Mississippi, for example. And there were not a lot of towns on the route that
I followed, passing about 40 miles south of Montgomery
and then flying direct to Meridian. The thing that fooled
me was a big forest fire that was apparently south of
course, with the smoke carried north across my route.
Given five miles visibility, I was supposed to see a little
town as a landmark at a predetermined time. But it was
not visible, and even the stars were hard to see. I knew
what caused this because the smoke of a forest fire has

108   an unmistakable smell. But knowing that wouldn't produce the town I wanted to see.

The immediate impulsive decision was to do something. But I managed to review the fact that I had been doing a good job of keeping the wings level and thus holding the correct heading, and I should just keep doing that. Soon the town was dimly visible through the murk, and in a short while I flew out of the smoke area and the visibility was back to normal. In retrospect, even though I didn't have a lot of instruments (or an instrument rating) I flew both those little airplanes at night mostly, if not solely, by reference to instruments. And because the objective was only to hold a heading, there was but one single measure of performance—keeping the wings level.

AIRLINE PADDLE

If I thought that I was doing it with a short paddle in the good old days, I wasn't alone. The airlines had only marginally better equipment. I was reminded of this one spectacular October day spent with the DC-3 that Piedmont Airlines restored for public relations activities.

Captain Bill Kyle, retired, was in charge of the DC-3 and told of the days when he flew the airplane on the line. There were only two airports with ILS systems on the Piedmont route structure, Norfolk and Cincinnati; all the rest of the approaches were based on a nondirectional beacon, a low-frequency range, or, in one case, a standard broadcast station. I don't know how the DC-3 panels were arranged then, but in the originals there was one set of flight instruments, right in the middle where the captain and copilot could see the instruments equally well, or equally unwell as the case may be.

They delivered the goods with this meager equip- **109**
ment, probably making schedules as well as you would
today with an equal number of nonprecision approaches along the way. And maybe this outlines one
of the big challenges. When Captain Kyle was maneuvering his DC-3 to land at night, with a crosswind, at the
completion of a nonprecision approach, he faced quite
a challenge. And faced it well, using a combination of
airmanship and good clear thinking combined with the
knowledge of what works and what doesn't work. The
other tools he worked with were basic. That has
changed, with a lot more electronic answers and solutions. But when you are circling to land at night you had
best have all the same ingredients that Captain Kyle
used in the late '40s and early '50s.

AWARE OF THE RISKS

One trait of a good pilot not recognized in the British
Airways testing is a bit negative but very necessary.
This is the full knowledge that if an airplane is improp-
erly used, it can be one of the most lethal machines in
the world. Airplanes can be exceedingly dangerous.
Ours is a society that seems to be intent on security
from cradle to grave. Warnings abound regarding everything on God's green earth, and they are peppered
through the pilot's operating handbook. But there are
still many warnings that are not given.

Perhaps most lacking is a warning in the area of
loss of control, especially in single-engine retractables
and light twins. What should the warning be? It should
be something to the effect that if lateral (roll) control of
the airplane is lost, in as few as 30 seconds the airplane
will be in a condition from which recovery is highly

110   unlikely. In a fully developed spiral dive, power on, the airplane is in what is best described as a vertical barrel roll and might reach a terminal velocity of 300 knots and a descent rate of 25,000 to 30,000 feet per minute. Tell me that isn't lethal. Yet we have pilots who oppose any requirement for backup instrument power or instrumentation in these airplanes. It is simply very dangerous to fly them without backups. The realistic pilot flies along always with the thought that if control is not maintained, you have but a few seconds in which recovery is possible. And there are other areas in flying that are completely unforgiving of any lapse of attention.

The basic hazards of flying have been brought home to me over the years by friends and acquaintances lost in airplanes. Virtually all were experienced pilots who got caught short in some basic area. The least experienced of the lot continued VFR into adverse weather. One tangled VFR with a thunderstorm. Two spun in. One lost control immediately after a night IFR departure; the airplane was so torn up that no determination of instrument or vacuum failure could be made. Two experienced pilots flew VFR into hillsides. Three (in the same airplane) spun in on a multiengine check ride. One lost control en route at night after an apparent problem with instrumentation. One ran out of gas at night. One had a midair collision. I learned very early that airplanes can and do kill people, and that while the risks can be minimized, they are always there, waiting patiently to surprise the pilot.

And, to me at least, the risks that can't be managed are very much offset by the rewards. With regard to those, I quote the greatest aviator of all, Charles Lindbergh: "I've flown for the love of flying, done the things I most wanted to do. . . . Why should man want to fly at all? . . . What justifies the risk of life? . . . I believe the

risks I take are justified by the sheer love of the life I   **111**
lead."*

THE OTHER GUY

Another challenge in flying is to understand the view-
point of the other person. Whether you are steamed up
about something that a writer or TV correspondent has
said about aviation, or about some delay or restriction
imposed by the air traffic control system, or what seems
to be an unreasonable stand by people in a segment of
aviation, it always helps to put yourself in the other
person's shoes.

Inbound to Trenton, New Jersey, one murky summer afternoon, I was getting the round-about routing
that is used to keep inbounds to Trenton from interfer-
ing with traffic at Philadelphia International. I was
headed north toward the DuPont Vortac at Wilmington,
Delaware, flying at 8,000 feet. A Learjet that had de-
parted one of the airports in the area was headed south
at 7,000, and its pilot was complaining mightily. He
wanted to climb because at 7,000 the fuel was literally
cascading out of the tanks and through the engines. The
controller tried to patiently explain to the pilot why he
could not climb, but this person was not easily convinced. Finally he asked if he was out of the Terminal
Control Area. When the controller responded that he
was indeed clear, the pilot, in a vindictive tone of voice,
said he was cancelling IFR, squawking 1200, and chang-
ing frequency. I assume that he rocketed up to 16,500
feet and turned southwestbound toward his destination. What he didn't know was that he was climbing

* From *The Last Hero: Charles A. Lindbergh* by Walter S. Ross,
published by Harper & Row.

112   through a high concentration of traffic (including my airplane) and that what he did was not only foolish, it was dangerous. Air traffic controllers don't give restrictions for fun, they do it for a reason.

A few days later, while having coffee in a motel room in Florida, I watched a TV program called "Crossfire" which was examining some of the problems of the air traffic control system. One of the principals on the show had a habit of interrupting the debate with his opinions. And he was particularly hard on air traffic controllers. When the matter of overtime was brought up, he opined that "they make a lot of money." Of course, this was show business, but I wished that he could have been in the airplane with me on the flight segment from over Patuxent, Maryland, up until the time I was handed off to Philadelphia Approach Control.

The controller was extremely busy. He really had more than he could handle, but he was doing a good job. When someone called in and wanted VFR advisories, he was polite and apologetic in telling the pilot that he didn't have time. The only crack in his armor came when he couldn't complete a handoff on a business jet and told the pilot to do a 360. The transmission was clear and not blocked, but the pilot did not acknowledge. Whether the pilot thought that by not answering he could go straight ahead and the controller would have to sort it out is open to question. But about a minute later the controller realized that the pilot had not complied with the instruction, and he made it known in no uncertain terms that this airplane had to begin a 360 immediately. No pilot likes to do a 360, but when the controller says to do one, it is for a valid reason and we have to understand that. And in this modern world, anybody who doesn't put on a little

extra fuel for the unexpected deviations and diversions   113
is not a very smart pilot.

MILITARY AIRSPACE

The inevitable and long diversions around military operating areas and other special-use airspace bother a
lot of us. To be perfectly honest, I was among the many
who felt that the military was just blocking off a lot of
airspace in case they wanted to use it. Then, on the kind
invitation of Lieutenant Kurt Koerner of the USAF, the
hospitality of Colonel John Jackson, and the good flying
of Captain Chris Miller, I had an opportunity to see
what the instructors and students at Williams Air Force
Base do with all those huge blocks of airspace to the
east and northeast of Phoenix, Arizona.

What they do is fly T-37s and T-38s in continuous
training during the hours of daylight. I had been exposed to military flying when I was in the Army, and on
some previous Air Force and Navy flights, but this was
my first shot at a T-38 and the ride gave me a new
understanding both of the thoroughness with which the
Air Force does its business, and their use of the airspace.

Thorough. There was a brief physical, a trip in the
altitude chamber and a complete briefing on the egress
and emergency procedures. They made sure that we
(my son was with me, and this lit his fire to be an Air
Force pilot but, sadly, his eyes wouldn't pass muster)
understood that a bird strike on the windshield would
probably incapacitate the front seat pilot and that it
would be our option to punch out or land the airplane
should that happen. The reference speeds were gone
over, and we each did three approaches and landings
in the simulator.

114   We went out in a four-ship formation. I was in the back seat with Chris Miller; Richard was in the back with Kurt Koerner. The other two airplanes had students Sheila O'Grady and Mike Jirik up front, instructors in the back.

The Air Force flies incredibly precise and tight formation. I do a lot of formation flying for photography in our magazine but these folks brought a new meaning to the term *tucked in.* And we were literally roaring around the sky, always turning to stay within the portion of the military operating area that was assigned for our use. It might look like a lot of airspace when you are flying around it at 170 knots, but it's awfully small at 500 knots. Air traffic control was monitoring our work and would call anytime we strayed near the edge of our airspace, which was defined by radials and distances off a Tacan station. With four T-38s a few feet apart, pulling three Gs in turns and formation maneuvers, it was obvious that there wouldn't be any way to see and avoid a slower airplane that might stray into the MOA. Beside helping me understand the other guy's point of view and need in the airspace system, it was no small thrill to be three feet away from my last-born, roaring around at 500 knots.

So there are a lot of challenges. They are what make it such a vibrant and enjoyable activity. Even if the weather is fine and the airplane perfect, the challenge is there to be precise in getting the airplane from here to there, making a perfect landing on arrival. Flying well is simply one of the most satisfying things that we can do.

5

Special
Relationships

THE MANNER in which we relate to the various factors in flying reveals a lot about our pilot-personality: Caring or careless? Work at proficiency or just get by? Study weather or depend on the briefer? Keep the airplane in top shape or have the minimum done under a shade tree? Fly when beat or always get a good rest the night before? Always there for aeronautical special events, or get your fill of flying on trips? Satisfied with minimum requirements as prescribed by the FAA, or look for more?

We all know that an airplane is not human, but machines as complex as these do have some human traits. And honestly, have you never patted your airplane on the cowling and thanked it for a nice ride, as you would a faithful horse? When you work on the airplane, even if only to clean the windows, do you feel a bond to it? I sure do. At this writing I have flown my

116 P210 4,300 hours—that's the better part of six months—
and you can't spend that much time without developing
a feel for the airplane. This feeling is one of the special
things about flying. Whether or not pilots who have it
are better than those who don't is open to question. But
there is bound to be something to the old saying "I won't
hurt you if you won't hurt me."

I know every sound the airplane makes. The slightest change will perk up my ears quickly and, usually, I
can tell the shop technicians what needs to be fixed and
what doesn't need to be fixed. And as the airframe ages,
I watch it very closely. Recently I found a tiny hairline
crack in the skin on the horizontal stabilizer. The shop
folks were surprised that I found this on a preflight, but
I have always been suspicious of tails, especially where
the elevators have trim tabs on them, and examine them
very thoroughly before flight. It surprised me a little that
this one was cracked because a lot of effort is put into
taking care of the tail. I avoid high-power runups on the
ground, which shake the tail, and can honestly say that
I have never stalled this airplane, which also shakes the
tail. So that crack came from below-normal use and
wear, and I'll watch the tail even more closely in the
future.

TAKEOFF

Knowing an airplane means that you can tell when you
are asking a lot of it. I saw a good example of this in
August 1987, while taking off at Green Bay, Wisconsin,
after attending the Oshkosh Air Show. Patrick Bradley,
Flying contributing editor, was flying and Phil Scott,
Flying associate editor, was in the back. A lot of baggage was on board and in total it was a pretty good
load. The day was hot and the wind was light but a bit

cross-downwind to the runway. Acceleration was sluggish at first and when Patrick rotated at 70 knots the nose lifted but the mains were determined to roll a bit longer. Once off, the airplane hesitated in ground effect, as if it didn't really want to go flying. If the sounds and the engine indications had not been normal, the performance was sluggish enough to make you think that there might be something wrong with the engine. But it gathered itself together and was soon climbing normally for a day with the temperature 20 degrees above standard and with a substantial load.

OVER WATER

I've always put a special effort into minimizing the risk of a water landing when flying across Lake Michigan. This is accomplished in the P210 by going across high —at a minimum of 16,000 feet and preferably higher. The point at which it would be best to go for the shore ahead instead of returning to the shore just left is always calculated, based on the wind aloft. Usually after a takeoff from Green Bay and a climb to either 17,000 feet or Flight Level 190, it works out, and the airplane is always within gliding distance of land. But this exceptionally hot day made me wonder and, indeed, there were a few moments in the middle of the lake where we would have been stuck with a water landing—near shore but probably farther than you'd want to swim. So I learned something about the relationship between 20 degrees above standard and a good load in the airplane. Next time I'll circle once on the climb to take out those vulnerable moments.

Knowing the airplane gives a pilot an advantage over water, or at night, or flying IFR. If you know the machine, there should be no "automatic rough." And

118 hopefully knowing it means that if anything is the slightest bit out of the ordinary, it will be investigated before flight. Early one morning another pilot started my airplane for what was to be the first leg of a long trip. The moment it started, I knew something was wrong. He wanted to run it awhile to see if it would straighten out, but I knew that it was running on five of six cylinders and wanted no part of starting a long trip when it had done this for the first time—even if it did run okay after a few minutes. The trouble turned out to be a badly cracked cylinder—one that you would not have wanted to take flying.

LONG WEEK

Watching Patrick fly the airplane home from Oshkosh was fun, too. He has flown my P210 more than any other airplane, and when he worked full-time for *Flying* we flew a lot together. The only person I have flown with more is my son Richard. The book Patrick and I did together, *Instrument Flying Refresher,* was in large part based on flying together. I watched him get his instrument, multiengine, and commercial, and progress to the point where he does a thoughtfully professional job of flying. And on this trip home from Oshkosh I was reminded of a project we did to measure the relationship between fatigue and pilot performance. Patrick cut his amount of sleep drastically for a few days while we were on a trip. He flew and I watched as his performance varied from very good to rather marginal. Most of the mistakes were relatively small, but if taken in just the wrong sequence they might have led to something major. There were some incorrect settings of frequencies and bearings, and he got out of phase with the airplane and a little wind shear on an approach to a

short field. But when one mag on the airplane decided   **119**
to quit and the engine belched a couple of times, he
really shaped up quickly.

The flight back from Green Bay relates to this because nobody has ever left Oshkosh without being at
least a little tired. We published a daily there, for the
EAA, and the hours were not exactly short. And then
there is the Acee Deucee, a classic corner tavern that
attracts an enthusiastic aviation crowd every night during the show. And in this particular year there was the
heat to wear you down during the day. So right after we
levelled off at FL190, Patrick asked if I would watch
over the airplane while he took a little snooze. He had
nodded off on the drive from Oshkosh up to Green Bay
as well, so I knew that he must be tired and that we
might learn more about fatigue and flying.

The snooze helped him, but it didn't stop him from
making some minor errors later on in the flight. One was
setting the OBS ten degrees off of where it should have
been. I mentioned it to him and he said it was correct.
Then he looked again and decided that it was not correct. In the interest of research I asked him if he could
remember what he was thinking about when he set it
incorrectly, but all he could think of was that he simply
misread the dial. That is an easy thing to do when you
are tired, and the relationship between a fatigued pilot
and the airplane has to be reckoned with.

GENTLY

A pilot who has the proper relationship with airplanes
treats them very gently. Whenever you hear a pilot talking about slamming, jamming, or ramming the throttle
or anything else on an airplane, you are hearing a pilot
who likely has a lot of trouble with his machinery. Air-

120 planes are made to be strong in some areas, but they are rather frail in others. They respond better to the gentle touch, too. Engines like to be kept as cool as possible and, when hot, don't like to be cooled suddenly. Brakes are really for emergencies, and to finish up the business of stopping once the power is at idle. In fact, I always wished that there was some way to prevent the use of brakes when the airplane is rolling unless the power is at idle. For some reason, pilots just love to ride the brakes.

The gentle business helps when you are flying, too. Rolling into turns gracefully instead of snappily gives the passengers a better ride. Making pitch changes slowly is the way to go. It is best to think of airplanes responding to pressures put on the controls rather than to gross movements of the controls. This is all part of forging a good relationship with airplanes. Like so many things it is not covered by any regulation, on any test, or even on most check rides. But it is important.

WEATHER

Weather is another area where the minimum we are required to learn leaves us without a good understanding of the relationship between airplanes and the elements. This is critical because what we do in airplanes is affected as much by weather as by anything else. And weather is not just clouds and rain or snow or fog. Weather might be heat, as at Green Bay on the flight related a few pages back.

Weather is also wind, as we found out at Tulsa one spring day. My son Richard was flying and there were four of us in the airplane, headed for the National Intercollegiate Flying Association airmeet in Colorado Springs. The elements were decidedly restless. There was a strong low just east of the front range of the Rockies with a resulting brisk southerly flow over Oklahoma. The automatic terminal information service recording at Tulsa reported that the wind was out of the south at 26 knots, gusting to 42. That's strong, but right down the runway.

I suggested to Richard that there had to be some wind shear because, from the groundspeed readout on the loran, we had a 70-knot tailwind on the downwind leg. On base the tower told us of a peak gust of 47 knots. On final, with only approach flaps, we calculated a good final approach speed to be 110 knots—90 would be normal with approach flaps, and we added the full 20 for the gusts. I told Richard to be ready for wind shear.

You don't see many like that one. As we descended through about 500 feet, the ground seemed to start rising up around us. The rate of descent had increased dramatically while the airspeed was decaying. Richard was hot on the power but it seemed to take a long time for it to be effective. The airspeed had dropped to 85 or 90 and when we came to a big bump that seemed to signify the end of the wind shear encounter, the stall horn bleated. The landing that followed was normal but the wind shear encounter had to be considered a significant encounter with "weather" on final approach.

Colorado in April

The flight from Tulsa on to Colorado Springs was relatively uneventful but with a weather lesson along the way. There was blowing dust all over the place, along with rainshowers in cumulus buildups. We started out at 14,000 feet, but soon climbed to FL200 in search of a smooth ride. Wrong. The ceiling at Colorado Springs was 9,500 feet above the ground so FL200 put us about

122   5,000 feet above the bases of bumpy clouds. I heard an American West 737 flying lower than I was and decided that he knew more about this than I did. We descended and had a relatively smooth ride below the cloud bases and above the dust.

The weather for the next few days had a significant impact on the NIFA flying activities, but we managed to complete the *Flying*-sponsored IFR event, operating from Colorado Springs instead of from the Air Force Academy airport, where the meet was being held. And when we awoke on Sunday morning, ready to head east toward home, three or four inches of snow had fallen. Colorado weather can indeed be fickle in late April. With the airplane cleaned off and three of Auburn's War Eagle Flying Team on board, we set out. The old man was flying. The War Eagles had hooted with the owls the night before and needed a nap.

A Real Storm

The low that had been in Colorado had moved and all the ingredients for a classic squall line were in place. The low was to the northeast of us with a strong cold front trailing, and the proper upper-level support was there in spades. The wind at 18,000 feet was forecast to be from 220 degrees at 77 knots. The storms were a couple of hundred miles to the east, and the only way to approach this sort of relationship between airplanes and weather is to go look, with plenty of gas and a resolve to go somewhere and land if a peaceful path through the weather can't be found.

Taxiing out, we were number two for departure behind none other than Richard L. Taylor of Ohio State University. Dick is also a Macmillan author and was flying a Cessna 340 this day. We have a special relation-

ship, too, both being named "Richard L." I have often   **123**
been asked to autograph his books and maybe the opposite is true. He headed off in a northeasterly direction, toward Ohio; we would be flying over Tulsa. Or at
least that is how the flight plan was filed.

The squall line was fully developed and ripping
along, spawning tornadoes and other delights, by the
time we reached it. There was no way to get through
it—a small gap was sighted around Oklahoma City, but
it was far from big enough for me to fly through. There
was a tornado sighting just a few miles north; it was the
sort of weather that's fun to look at, but only from a
distance.

We stopped in at Ardmore, Oklahoma, for some
fuel. The surface wind was very strong behind the
squall line and there was blowing dust in the air. After
that, we continued paralleling the line of storms until
we reached a good-sized gap in the line down around
Waco, Texas. From there it was a clear shot to Auburn.
I flew on home to New Jersey that night, in good
weather.

Zig or Zag

There was a lot of distance to cover on that flight and
it was clear that a direct route wasn't going to work. The
best direction for a diversion was obvious, too. The low
was north of course and strong. The farther south we
flew, the farther away from the low we'd be. While that
doesn't guarantee anything, it gave the best chance of
finding gaps in the line of thunderstorms. As strong as
that low was, the only other possibility I would have
explored would have been a trip well around the north
side of it. As a cold front overtakes a warm front and
forms an occlusion, the weather can become positively

124 violent, even well away from precipitation. That was a strong low, one for me to stay well south of for the route I was flying this day. There would have been a lot of low IFR and probably a lot of ice to the north of it, so if that route had been chosen, it would have had to be with extra care and good alternatives. That's a rather complex relationship between the airplane, a weather system, and geography and, that day at least, understanding the relationship made possible the completion of the trip, if a little later than anticipated.

BUSTED FORECAST

That day the weather was just about as forecast. The low and the front and the squall line all followed the script. But this isn't always the case. It simply isn't possible for the forecasters to hit it on the button every time.

A pilot once asked how pilots could be expected to exercise good weather judgment when the forecasts are often so inaccurate. That is rather simple. An airplane is the best weather sensor in the world, and any pilot who is surprised by a busted forecast is not doing his job while flying along. If a problem with a forecast compromises the safety of a flight, it's strictly the pilot's fault because, regardless of the circumstances, the pilot is in command. It's hard to envision the forecasting problem that would back a pilot into a corner from which there would be no hope for escape.

Busted forecasts and less than completely accurate information work both ways. I got a briefing for a Myrtle Beach, South Carolina, to Vero Beach, Florida, flight that said nothing about thunderstorms or other bad things. Before I had flown 200 miles there was a tornado watch posted for the area ahead. It didn't affect the

safety of the flight. To pout over the bad forecast would   125
have done exactly no good. What I saw was what I got;
avoiding the storms that were developing in the area
was a matter of a few minor deviations.

On the other hand, a convective sigmet that told of
a line of thunderstorms between the nose of my airplane and Wichita, Kansas, was something to think
about. These had been forecast and they were apparently being delivered. But, using the radar and the
Stormscope in my airplane, it was possible to determine
that a slight deviation north of course would take us
through an area with no electrical activity and only light
rain. The sigmet had been incorrect in labelling the
whole line as thunderstorms, as was witnessed by our
smooth passage through the line. The decisions that are
made on the flight deck far outweigh the importance of
forecasts.

FOGGY DAY

The relationship of fog to flying is one place where a lot
of us tempt the fates. Up front, it has to be acknowledged that forecasting the time that fog will lift is extremely difficult. Even though they say that it might be
clear by nine, conditions might remain foggy for the
whole day. Or it might clear up by eight. Fog comes in
a wide variety of thicknesses: the surface temperature,
the temperature aloft, general circulation, and the presence of higher clouds can all affect when it lifts.

I fly from Trenton, New Jersey, to Indianapolis, In-
diana, frequently, and it is always interesting when the
weather is bad. For the months when the wind blows
strongly out of the west, my airplane holds enough fuel
to make Indianapolis with a close alternate. I use Mount
Comfort airport, east of the city, as a frequent stop. If

126   the wind is howling aloft, the only feasible alternate is often Indianapolis International, across town. The accuracy of a "fog lifting by nine" forecast becomes very important.

That was the case one December morning with fog at Indianapolis but with a forecast of 25,000 scattered and three miles until 1600Z, with the visibility then increasing to seven miles. If the forecast was right, it looked like a good deal for a 1230Z departure for Mount Comfort with Indianapolis as the alternate.

The fog was far more serious than was forecast this morning. As I flew along making notes on weather, it was quite obvious that the original plan had to be discarded even though the forecast still said that Indianapolis would be improving any minute now—certainly by the time I would get there. But the runway visual range was 600 feet, and flying toward that with not a lot more than the minimum legal fuel is a way to create genuinely anxious moments.

Columbus, Ohio, which might have been considered first as a place to stop for fuel, was zero-zero with the runway visual range well below minimums. Dayton, a little closer to Indy, had minimums: runway visual range 2,600 variable 3,500. Cincinnati, a bit to the south, had about the same. Dayton's forecast was a lot better than its weather, but at least they had minimums. So Dayton became my destination, even though it would have been legal to continue to Mount Comfort because the Indy forecast was still for it to have alternate minimums.

The forecast was amended, finally, but it was still overly optimistic in forecasting an improvement to VFR conditions by 1600Z. I stopped at Dayton, bought fuel, and when I passed south of Indianapolis at 1735Z they were still reporting zero-zero with the RVR well below

minimums. In fact, it stayed that way all day. While a   127
continuation to Mount Comfort, a missed approach
there, and then over to Indy as an alternate fit the text-
books, only the completion of a potentially deadly
below-minimums approach would have saved the day
had I done that. The relationship between fog and IFR
pilots is indeed complex.

NEW LOW

Another trip, this one from Auburn, Alabama, to New
Jersey, showed how the formation of a new low-pressure area can change the nature and progress of a flight.

The forecast wind at 24,000 feet was from 240 degrees at 96 knots and I was looking forward to a really
fast trip. The best groundspeed I had seen in the P210
was 308 knots, east of Albuquerque in the wintertime,
and I thought maybe the wind this day might be a little
stronger than forecast and I could best that at FL230.

The flying was fine, but the wind was only boosting
the groundspeed to the 270–280 range. Nothing to com-
plain about but no record. And the view ahead was not
good. What appeared to be snow showers that were
forming over the Appalachians and drifting eastward
were ahead, and the tops looked higher than FL230.
Would it be rough in them? Probably, though there probably wouldn't be a lot of ice.

Then, however, a pilot report added a new dimension. Northeast of Richmond severe turbulence was
being reported from 17,000 feet up to Flight Level 230.
The reporting aircraft was a 727, and if it was serious
to them, what would it be to my little green airplane?
Something was obviously brewing. What happened
was the movement of a jet core over the area that
spawned the formation of a new surface low to the

128   southwest of Richmond. The low was extremely strong and did a lot of damage in northeastern North Carolina. My solution was to descend to 13,000 feet to be well below the lowest altitude where the 727 reported the really bad stuff.

It was plenty bumpy in the descent, made with the landing gear down, but the air was relatively smooth at 13,000. The big surprise came when I looked at the groundspeed. It was 175 knots, or about 100 knots lower than it had been at Flight Level 230. The wind at the higher altitude was out of the southwest; at the lower altitude it was out of the southeast, driven by the surface low to the south. That is a lot of wind shear and it was apparently worse to the northeast, where the 727 was flying.

SEASONS

We who fly have a different relationship to seasons from that of nonpilots. The seasonal changes make flying more interesting and vice versa. Airports, for whatever reason, are the hottest places in the summer, the coldest in the winter, and, to make up for this, they can be the prettiest places in the spring and fall.

For no particularly good reason, the flying year for me has always started in the fall. Maybe that's because I first soloed in the fall, or maybe it is because that first strong cold front that whips through offers such a clear indication of a coming change in the weather. Summer is gone. It all depends on where you live, too. Since starting to fly, I have lived in only two places long enough to develop what might be called a feel for the local weather—Arkansas for 15 years and New Jersey for 22 years. But I have flown all over the country in all seasons, so I have had some exposure to all areas. If a

pilot carefully considers wind, terrain, sources of mois- 129
ture, and the actual and forecast surface and upper-
level conditions, plus the season of the year, there's no
reason to be surprised anywhere. For example, I mentioned that late April snow in Colorado. I have been
there enough times to know that anything can happen
anytime.

When the flying year starts in September or October, depending on where you live, conditions are generally very pleasant. In the fall, weather tends to change
reasonably quickly so if it's bad, patience is a great
virtue. It's in the fall that we are reminded of what
strong headwinds can do to progress across the ground,
and the average groundspeed for trips drops because
we spend more time flying in strong headwinds than we
spend flying with strong tailwinds. Along the east coast
there's always a refresher on what a nor'easter brings.
The ultimate nor'easter, a hurricane, might blow by
anywhere from Maine to Brownsville, Texas. There's a
lot of truly nice weather early, but by November the
serious IFR sets in.

The first really cold snap, or snow, always comes
as a shock. There is just no way to remember from year
to year all the little things that change when the
weather decides to do its wintertime business. Snow
fouls up airports, cold makes airplanes hard to start,
every bit of frost has to be removed before flight, and
airframe icing en route is always a problem.

Snow

Snow is something that demands extra thought, too,
because it can close an airport as quickly as fog. For a
trip from Myrtle Beach, South Carolina, to Trenton,
New Jersey, I had in my hot hand a Philadelphia fore-

130   cast for 3,000 overcast variable 1,000 overcast in light
snow with a risk of 500 obscured and one mile in snow.
That wouldn't do as an alternate for Trenton (for which
a forecast was unavailable), so Baltimore, which was
forecasting better conditions, went on the sheet as the
alternate.

Flying along and checking weather revealed that
the snow was more aggressive than was forecast. Philly
was 300 obscured and three-quarters; Trenton was 100
obscured and a half, both in snow. It was cold, 23° F, so
I decided that any snow just had to be light. The classic
smothering snows usually come when the temperature
is a little warmer, in the 28 to 31 range. One thing I didn't
consider was the temperature aloft. It was ten degrees
above standard at 15,000 feet, or, at −5° C, the same as
on the ground. (Why can't aviation use the same measure of temperature on the surface and aloft?) Tempera-
tures above standard mean the atmosphere can hold,
transport, and deposit more moisture, but I didn't give
that a lot of thought. It hadn't been snowing long, either.

Trenton was still 100 and a half in snow when I
neared the area, and while the visibility was at minimums, if there was a 100-foot ceiling instead of just
obscurement in snow, there might be no view of the
runway at the decision height. But I was going to have
plenty of fuel for the trip to the alternate, or even to a
farther away alternate, so it appeared prudent to shoot
the ILS at Trenton.

The approach worked okay, the runway was in
sight from a little above the decision height, but the
airport looked a mess. The plows hadn't been out yet
and the tower said the runways and taxiways were all
snow-covered. In fact, about four inches of snow was
on the ground. This posed no problem landing, but taxiing took a lot of power and it took a lot of help to get

the airplane into the T-hangar. The drive home was treacherous. So what is the moral to the story? The airport was closed for snow removal right after we landed, was closed for quite a while, and closed several more times before the storm passed. Snow can close an airport as effectively as fog.

And even where the runways are cleared, the effects of snow can close an airport or a runway. One foggy day over West Virginia one of the airports with minimums and an ILS was doing a brisk business until a pilot misjudged a turnoff and got stuck with his tail sticking out over part of the runway. They had no choice but to close the airport until the airplane was moved.

One more snow story. Some years ago my friend Johnny Hecker and I were going to Albuquerque to the wedding of his brother-in-law. The trip was made in Johnny's Vultee BT-13, a surplus World War II trainer that lived on noise and copious amounts of fuel. We got stuck for a day in Amarillo, Texas, in a snowstorm. When the sky cleared and we went to the airport to leave, the airport manager told us we could not take off because the airport was closed. I think she was confident that we couldn't leave because awakening that 450 horsepower Pratt & Whitney from its cold sleep wasn't going to be easy.

We were persistent cusses, though, and intended to leave. And we must have uncovered some bad vibes between the tower and airport management for when we inquired if they would clear us for takeoff if we got things going, the tower operator said, "Sure." As far as he was concerned the airport was open. I had to hand-prop the old 450 to get it going but it was soon chugging and Johnny and I were ready to go. With its big tires, the BT-13 had no problem in the snow and we officially "opened" the closed airport by taking off.

And Colder

Those very cold days are a sign that winter has become vengeful. By very cold I mean 10° F or less. Airplanes with piston engines have to be preheated, even if they are using multigrade oil, and preflight inspections are painful. But the weather is usually clear, and an early-morning look at the frozen landscape is a special treat for a pilot. I remember flying along one day trying to decide whether to stop at Dayton or Indianapolis, basing the decision on the surface temperature. I would naturally pick the warmest place. But then I started thinking about how silly I was being. I don't remember the exact values, but one was something like −10° and the other −8°. Would I or the airplane have known the difference?

Farther South

In the lower third of the U.S. winter has an entirely different meaning to the aviator. There is cold weather there, to be sure, and I remember spending hours getting my Cardinal RG pried out of my hangar at North Little Rock, Arkansas, to fly to Wichita one January day. There had been a humongous amount of snow, all the interstates were closed, all the big airports were closed, and everything was at a standstill. It was almost eerie to fly up the Arkansas River valley, over eastern Oklahoma, and into Kansas without seeing anything moving. Except for one thing. Some fine farmer was out on a horse, galloping around the fields. I'll always remember the sight, and wondering who was having the most fun—me looking at him riding his horse, or him riding his horse. Not only was I the first to leave the Little Rock

area after the storm, three days later I was the first to   133
land in the area.

But a storm like that is the exception rather than
the rule in the south. What usually happens there is that
a cold front pushes down while the low-pressure area
that is supporting it moves off to the northeast. The
circulation around the low weakens and the front stops.
How far south it stops depends on the strength and
location of the low. Then the front remains stationary
until the upper-level support for the development of a
new low comes along, and another storm system is
born. I don't know that this is supported by meteorological evidence, but it seems to me the low that brings the
front that stops usually develops in Colorado, just east
of the Rockies. The second low that forms on the stationary front comes to life in the Gulf of Mexico. Then
another forms in Colorado, then another in the Gulf, and
on and on all winter.

The point is that when a front stops in the winter,
the weather can be bad for quite a while. And it often
does this at times people like to go places, Thanksgiving
and Christmas for example.

Spring Springs

The first time you hear the words *tornado* or *hail* or
surface wind gusts to 60 knots, you know that springtime has probably come. Spring brings a lot of good
things, but for the pilot it also brings a lot of weather
with which it is difficult to form a meaningful relationship. The fronts that stall do so a bit farther to the north,
and if you fly from a grass airport in parts of the country
where the ground freezes, you become very familiar
with mud. Cold fronts can be very strong in the spring

134 but, fortunately, the air behind them just isn't as cold as a few months earlier.

Crazy Days of Summer

The summertime is probably every pilot's favorite time to fly—if for no reason other than it's vacation time and we get to fly places and do things that people without airplanes have a difficult time doing. Thunderstorms are usually scattered, or at least arranged in manageable batches, and the tops of the haze are usually below the ceiling of our airplane. There are weather systems in the summer, but they aren't usually as clearly defined as in other seasons.

The places we fly for fun tend to have the shortest runways, and of course we want to go there on the warmest days and take as many people as possible. That puts a requirement for extra care on the pilot. Summertime is a good time to limit loads—fuel, bodies, and baggage—when flying from a vacation spot's 2,500-foot strip.

My wife and I always try to go to a different place every time, taking best advantage of the airplane's flexibility. Block Island, Rhode Island, offshore south of Providence and just east of Long Island, New York, is a neat place to visit for a short while. The way the airplane and airport were used is a good example of the difference in our summer and winter flying. I seldom fly my airplane with as many as four on board. Guess how many went to Block Island. I seldom use runways 2,500 feet long. Guess the length of the Block Island runway. You were right in both cases. Maybe that's why they don't sell gas at Block Island, to get pilots to take off a bit lighter. There's nothing wrong with either the load or

the runway length, but because it is a relationship that   135
is not made familiar by frequent exposure, a good review in advance is required.

REVIEW

And mention of a review is a good place to start the
examination of the pilot's relationship with training and
proficiency flying. A good relationship here is critical,
lest an individual's flying become a very high-risk
event.

When we learn how to fly in order to get our tickets,
we really learn very little about flying. The real education starts at the completion of training, as we try to put
this newly learned skill to some use. And if a pilot stays
in the training process, upgrading certificates and ratings until he has them all, and spending relatively big
bucks on proficiency maintenance, there's a good
chance that the pilot can make it all the way through a
flying career without serious incident. But a pilot who
goes for the minimum training and then does nothing
more than a biennial flight review every two years
might well become one of our unfortunate statistics.

As this is written, a general aviation industry group
is drafting a petition to the FAA to require type-specific
training in high-performance singles and light twins.
Some will no doubt oppose this. But it is justified. Look
at it this way: There are perhaps 17,000 Bonanzas and
Cessna 210s flying in the U.S. Every week there is a fatal
accident in a Bonanza or a 210, for a total of 52 a year.
There are 170,000,000 motor vehicles in the U.S. There
are four more zeroes in the motor vehicle number so if
they had fatal accidents in the same proportion as
Bonanzas and 210s you'd have to add four zeroes to 52,

136 to come up with 520,000 motor vehicles in fatal wrecks every year. The actual number is somewhere around 30,000 or a little less.

Anyone who does not acknowledge that as a serious problem is kidding himself. So how do we go about fixing this? Training and proficiency flying is the answer. And what do you train to? Perfection, which is what the next chapter is all about.

6

The Perfect Flight!

ONCE A YEAR Sporty's Pilot Shop, Cessna, Flight-Safety International, Jeppesen-Sanderson, *Flying*, and a number of individuals pitch in to make possible an IFR flying contest for the National Intercollegiate Flying Association. The drill is to have the contestants fly a normal IFR flight, in the system if possible. Scoring is done by noting the number of times the contestant strays from the straight and narrow. The FAA check ride standards are used, altitude within 100 feet for example, and the number of points assigned for each infraction is doubled after the contestant passes the final approach fix inbound. There is no question that they compete intent on flying the perfect flight. And while you might feel that going flying with a bunch of yahoos from the industry and an aviation magazine would be intimidating, the fact that we do occasionally see perfect flights puts this to rest.

After judging for ten years, flying with perhaps 60 contestants in that time, I have seen a few that could go

138   in the book as perfect. And I was genuinely proud to have been able to fly with a young person so dedicated to flying well. I have also felt privileged for the exposure to all the rest, most of whom flew well if not perfectly, and to have run across them in following years, to hear their stories of success in the aviation business. Airline pilots, corporate pilots, military pilots, and key people in aviation businesses—they all give a strong impression of being those who want to do the very best.

PERFECT SNOWSTORM

One of the perfect flights was flown in the Colorado snowstorm mentioned in the last chapter. It was a day that would put pressure on any pilot. We had had to move the event to Colorado Springs from the Air Force Academy because of weather, so the onus was on the contestants to seek us out for a ride in the van we rented for transport back and forth. Because all the other flying events were cancelled, the contestants had the time to do this, and we drew a good crowd. Despite weather and logistics, we flew 31 of the 35 who were scheduled.

The weather at Colorado Springs was bad—ranging all the way down to 200 and a half in snow—but it was pretty good at Denver so we decided to fly as long as Denver remained a gold-plated alternate. Some of the contestants were bothered by the weather, others were not. Especially the winner, Lori Laushkin of Mount San Antonio College in California. I flew with her and she conducted a virtually perfect flight. After we landed, with a half-mile visibility in snow, I told her she had to be careful of one thing. Apprehensive, she asked what that was. I told her that on an ILS approach she had best watch the flags on the ILS indicator very closely because she had kept the needles so perfectly

aligned on the approach that if the ILS or the receivers   139
in the aircraft quit, she would only notice by the flags.

ANOTHER BAD WEATHER DAY

Another year I flew with a bright young pilot who got
completely confused, and this was equally interesting.

The contestant's first problem was that he got lost.
We were in a rather bucolic air traffic control environment, and when I asked the manager of the facility how
far we could let them stray, he said that they would
watch us and not to worry—they would tell us when the
contestant had strayed too far. This pilot compounded
his navigational errors and was having difficulty con-
trolling the airplane. Simply, he was far behind the
swoop and dip curve.

The weather was grungy, and I suspected that the
juicy clouds we were flying in were the first that this
pilot had ever flown in despite the fact that he had an
instrument rating, as all our contestants do. When the
pilot was finally convinced that he had no knowledge
of the location of the airplane, and had no ideas about
how to figure out present position, he asked the controller where he was. In the true spirit of competition, the
controller said, "No, you are in that contest, I'm not
about to tell you where you are." I knew where he was,
that he was having trouble with both navigation and
control, and that he hadn't a chance of scoring anywhere except close to last place. So it was time to see
if it would be possible to make the flight worth something other than a bad taste in his mouth.

I showed him where we were on the chart and
suggested that this would be a good time for him to try
to fly a perfect ILS approach. The weather was fairly
low at the airport, with a mile visibility or a bit less in

140   rain. The controller agreed to vector us to the final approach course.

At first the pilot was jerking the airplane around and wasn't doing a particularly good job of tracking the localizer outside the marker. Finally, with some gentle cajoling, I got him to settle down and fly a heading—the correct heading will get you there every time. Fly the heading and see what the needle does. Fly a rate of descent and see what the glideslope does. Then make the small adjustments that are necessary to keep the needles still and centered. Down we came. He got with the program and in the end the approach was very good. I left him with the thought that he could do very well, but that he had to learn never to lose track of position, and to develop the ability to tell himself the same things that I had told him to calm down the approach. That was all he needed.

MORE THAN ONE WAY

When I leave NIFA, I always grade a few of my own flights. Often, it isn't a pretty sight. After many of the meets the first leg toward home was flown by my son, and I'd grade him. He competed for four years and placed second twice but the perfect flight was elusive for him, too. Then he started flying in a different environment, working for FlightSafety International at Dothan, Alabama, teaching U.S. Army helicopter pilots how to fly fixed-wing aircraft. Where his previous flight instructing had been in a good general aviation environment, the military is different. There is stronger discipline and greater demand for perfection. One way: the Army Way. On a daily basis he demanded performance from his students and I was looking forward to an 800-nautical-mile flight that we would fly together. Before

takeoff I challenged him to fly the perfect flight and said
that I was going to make a list of every transgression.

After 800 nautical miles I had a blank sheet of
paper. And we had only one discussion about an item
of technique. On the return to Dothan we had below-
VFR weather and were vectored for an ILS approach.
The controller turned us on a long final, following a
Cessna Conquest. Richard said it was their procedure
to have the airplane stabilized for the approach at the
marker inbound. That is the airline way to do it as well.
But it doesn't always work well in light airplanes at
busy airports, especially when they ask you to keep the
speed up for as long as possible. So I developed one
procedure that keeps things moving, and one that *really*
keeps things moving. I suggested the moderate approach for this ILS. Over the marker at 150 indicated,
gear down, approach flaps, power back to 15 inches.
The airplane then decelerates to full flaps speed while
tracking the glideslope. Flaps down at 115 and the
speed then bleeds back to 80 by the time the runway is
reached. That is not a stabilized approach, but it is a
procedure. I could tell that Junior felt the Army way to
be the better way, but if he ever goes to Washington
National, he'll be the most unpopular pilot of the day if
he flies an 80-knot approach from the marker to the
airport.

What does a perfect flight prove? Nothing really,
other than that the pilot paid 100-percent attention
throughout the flight. And perhaps this is important.
Perhaps paying attention is what makes us fly well.
Perhaps it is also what we can do to keep some influence, such as fatigue, from compromising the safety of
a flight.

Altitude: The airplane has to be at some altitude,
so why not precisely at the correct altitude? Nobody is

142   ever going to accuse you of anything for straying up 80 feet and down 80 feet. But why do it? It sure isn't required and the satisfaction that comes from keeping the altimeter bang-on is nice.

Heading: As long as the wind and the true airspeed remain constant, flying a constant heading will result in a constant ground track. The challenge is to find that heading and then fly it with precision. And it needs to be found gently, lest you stitch up the airway, adding extra miles to the trip.

Airspeed: There is always a correct one, begging to be flown.

Awareness of Position: This one is especially important because if you fly the airplane into a mountain while holding the altitude, heading, and airspeed with great stability, the flight will hardly be deemed perfect.

COMBINATION OF INGREDIENTS

When flying any airplane we might, before takeoff, go over everything that is available in that airplane as well as the characteristics of the airplane. Then the meteorology of the day has to be applied to complete the combination. Only with the specifics in mind can we have a shot at that perfect flight. And, in retrospect, the judging of whether or not a person keeps the heading within 10 degrees of correct is far more subjective than the judging of altitude, which is an absolute, as is airspeed with appropriate adjustments for unusual conditions.

Back in the terrible old days when many airplanes didn't have navigational radios, we drew out wind triangles (or used an E-6B) before every flight and determined what heading would be flown for each leg based on the wind, the magnetic variation, and the compass deviation. It was done precisely, to the degree, before setting off. Every time. This gave us a leg up on today's pilots who, because most navigation is done with electronics, seldom take off with the calculated knowledge that there will be probably ten degrees left drift, for example. The tendency is to think only in terms of the effect the wind will have on groundspeed.

Flying along with a relatively new pilot one day, I watched as he fooled with the heading. Ten left, 20 right, 15 left, each adjustment caused by some slight motion of the nav needle. I mentioned that there was one heading there somewhere that would work. If he would consider the wind (which hadn't been done at all), estimate the heading that would work, fly that heading, and adjust it only five degrees at a time in response to the reaction of the nav needle to the new heading, he'd be able to find the number that would take us where we were going. He apparently was not aware that the Northstar M-1 loran in the airplane gives the ground track being made—an item of information that will get you to the correct heading quicker than anything else. With it you have only to fly a heading, look at the track being made, look at the desired track, and then make a heading correction for the difference.

FROM THE GROUND

Watching the loran, it is possible to predict when a controller is going to call with the suggestion that the airplane is straying from the straight and narrow. More than once I have told the pilot flying that the controller will be calling shortly, asking what is going on. Then the controller calls. "How did you know?" is the next question from the pilot. Simple. If the airway is 283 degrees, the pilot is off a little, and makes a big correction, and

144   the ground track becomes something like 250, as seen on the loran, it's going to appear strange to the controller. He has a feature on his radar that projects the aircraft track ahead, based on what it is doing at the moment. If the target is close to the airway but the track is 30 degrees off, he doesn't know what it is that you might be trying to do.

Another heading item relates to what happens when you pass a VOR or other fix, and a turn and change in track is required. Say, for example, you are flying a heading of 080 to track 090, and after passing the VOR the track for the new airway becomes 105. A majority of pilots would turn to 105 after passing the VOR: A much better starting point would be 95. The wind drift correction used on the previous leg should be approximately the same for the new leg. Flying precisely perfect flights is a matter of putting the required thought into the proceedings.

AIRSPEED

Airspeed plus or minus some knots is another measure of the perfect flight, and is a big determinant in getting the proper performance out of the airplane. Airspeeds are commonly referred to as "V" speeds, which simply identifies the velocity for various things. On takeoff, the first one in a single is Vr, the speed at which you rotate the aircraft for liftoff. The next would be Vx or Vy, which are the speeds for the best angle of climb or the best rate of climb.

Say takeoffs are made with 10-degree flaps, Vr is 70 knots, and the best rate-of-climb speed at cruise climb power is 110 with the flaps up. What's the best way to get the airplane from 70 to 110? There's no chance of flying a perfect flight if in advance you don't have a plan in mind to do that. The plan would have to include a nose-up pitch attitude to be flown in that first segment of the climb—an attitude that will let the airplane accelerate smoothly from 70 to 110 while the configuration is being changed. Then, once at 110, the power can be reduced to cruise climb.

The control of pitch attitude, and thus airspeed, in this first segment climb is more challenging in some airplanes than in others. Aircraft of certain configurations—T-tails and long wheelbases stand out—require more elevator force for liftoff than is required to maintain the desired pitch attitude. Thus if the nose is pulled briskly to 10 degrees nose-up, with no further elevator pressure added, the nose will go on up past 10 degrees. On these aircraft, back pressure has to be relaxed as the target pitch attitude is neared, lest it be overshot with resulting low airspeed and poor acceleration. On some jets this actually involves what seems like a push forward as the desired pitch attitude is neared.

FLYING CHARACTERISTICS

There are times when we might fly an airplane and feel that the flying qualities make it difficult to fly a perfect flight. Certainly all airplanes are not alike in the way they fly. I remember one day in an MD-80 simulator when the instructor induced a surging engine right after takeoff. The characteristics of the airplane were such that I flew it into an interesting dutch roll maneuver that looked pretty bad. I did finally manage to fly out of it, but that is definitely a characteristic of that airplane that I would have to learn before being comfortable with it. This is also true of pitch changes with flaps extension, the characteristic of airplanes with the main gear located too far aft to be prone to over-rotation on

146 takeoff, and other flying qualities that we find in some but not all airplanes. If we can't learn these things, then I guess we shouldn't call ourselves pilots. Some airplanes require a very fine touch on the controls, others require some muscle.

EN ROUTE SPEED

Control of cruising speed is not critical and is done in many ways. Some pilots, more likely military pilots, always fly with a target indicated cruising airspeed and set the power to fly at that speed. Concorde flies with a speed target, Mach 2 at cruise, with the power levers full forward and because it is alone above the rest of the jets, the altitude is allowed to increase as the aircraft becomes lighter with fuel burn-off. In others, pilots think in terms of percentages of power.

I usually set cruise power based on fuel flow, because that is an indication of how much power is being used. And the fuel flow is selected based on the wind and the length of the flight. If the tanks are verified as completely full by visual examination, my P210 flies four hours at 100 pounds per hour; for each five pounds off the fuel flow, add 15 minutes to the time the airplane can be flown and landed with one hour's fuel in the tanks. So setting power by fuel flow rather than airspeed makes life simpler for me in this airplane. And most of us just don't worry over airspeed control en route, because whatever power we normally use keeps the airspeed in the green.

COMING DOWN

The speed to maintain in a descent depends on a lot of things, and it's often possible to get an argument going about whether or not it is wise to fly with the airspeed in the yellow arc, which is identified as being approved for smooth air operation only. Personally, I use top of the green, Vc, in smooth air only and back off to Vc minus ten knots when it gets bumpy. If it's really bumpy, then Va, maneuvering speed, is the correct one unless your aircraft specifies a turbulent air-penetration speed.

Speed control in a descent is an important matter of pilot technique. Speed comes from attitude and power. If a pilot who is five knots slow sticks the nose down another five degrees to get the speed up, and holds it there until the speed is on a proper value, the speed will go well past the proper value. The key to speed adjustments in a descent, or at any other time, is to watch the rate at which a correction makes the airspeed change. The rate of change in the airspeed tells you how much you need to lead the further correction that will be made as the airspeed nears the correct value.

Vf or Vfe, the maximum-design flaps speed or maximum-design flaps extended speed, must be considered and heeded along with Vlo, the maximum landing gear operating speed, and Vle, the maximum landing gear extended speed.

When you get to the approach, the key speed is Vref. While the Army and others might want approaches flown at that speed, or at that speed plus a certain value, the real importance of Vref is in the pilot knowing where he is in relation to it. If Vref is calculated at 1.3 times the stalling speed of the airplane, it likely seems low to many light-airplane pilots. Stalling speed decreases with weight and in a Cessna 210 at what might be a typical arrival weight, full flaps Vref might be as low as 68 knots. Few people make approaches in 210s at that speed and as a result most 210

148   landings follow a little float and most result in a touchdown that is well above stalling speed. Certainly a pilot
should know that if he is below Vref with the wings
level, or below Vref plus five in normal maneuvering
turns (up to 30 degrees), the airplane is very near to
trouble and steps should be taken to improve the speed
margin above the stall.

On the other hand, the amount above Vref tells the
pilot what manner of difficulty is being built into the
landing. Certainly crossing the fence at a speed that is
more than ten knots above Vref will result in either a
long float or a very level landing. Only the likelihood of
strong low-level wind shear would be a reason for anything more than Vref plus ten on short final. If the field
is short and the pilot expects to come anywhere close
to the landing distance figures in the pilot's operating
handbook, it had best be precisely on either the calculated Vref or, if there is one, the short-field approach
speed listed in the pilot's operating handbook.

The other measure of a proper approach is pitch
attitude. There is a correct attitude for a normal approach. Is it flown, constantly, or is the approach such
that the pilot is diddling with the power and attitude all
the way in?

AWARENESS OF POSITION

Where those other items in the perfect flight are quan-
tifiable in terms of instrument readings, the pilot's
awareness of position is less clear. It's possible to fly
along and tell that a pilot is holding the airplane steady.
All that's required is a look at the instruments. But only
the pilot knows if he is totally aware of the position of
the airplane in relation to all the things that count. This
is like having a mental DME and radar altimeter that

constantly reviews the distance to fly and the altitude   **149**
above the ground, and then relates it to the readings on
the instrument panel.

This really becomes critical when the action heats
up toward the end of the flight. A pilot who doesn't keep
a constant tab on the flying miles to go before reaching
the runway, and the height above the ground beneath as
well as above the runway threshold, is not likely to
make a graceful arrival. If, when leaving an airport in
mountainous terrain, a pilot is not aware enough of
where he is (in the mountains) to become curious
enough to look up and fly the published departure procedure, then the airplane's position in relation to the
terrain might become precarious.

In maneuvering for an instrument approach, the
controller usually tells us which heading to fly. But if we
don't keep a constant tab on the position of the airplane
in relation to the localizer and glideslope—as well as
the speed, heading, altitude, and configuration of the
airplane—then there might be surprises. The pilot who
constantly reviews position—"Here I am, here is how it
relates to everything else"—just has an easier time nib-
bling away at that perfect flight.

We have to also be aware of the attitude of the
airplane, and a fine touch is required on a departure as
well as arrival. On departure, it's simple. There is one
pitch attitude to fly after takeoff and the only trouble
most folks have with this is in airplanes where the
amount of pull required to lift the airplane off the runway, if maintained, will result in the pitch attitude exceeding the desired value. That's just a matter of flying.

On final approach, an awareness of attitude is an
integral part of landing. Say, for example, a pilot decides the airspeed is five knots high and reduces power
a little and raises the nose to correct this. The attitude

150   is thus not that of a normal approach. If this condition is left alone, the airspeed will decrease by the desired five, and will then decrease below the desired value unless the attitude is changed again. Where the rub comes is when the airplane crosses the fence in an attitude other than the correct one. If the nose is too high, the airplane is slowing and the hit could be a hard one. If the nose is too low, the airspeed is probably fast and the landing will either be prolonged or in a level attitude—neither of which signals the end of a perfect flight.

ATTENTION TO DETAIL

Along the way there are a lot of details to take care of if an airplane is to be flown well. On a trip I made a list of the details that were missed along the way; each represents something worthy of attention. Each was a deviation from the perfect flight.

When flying with another pilot, good crew coordination calls for certain actions. One crew procedure that we can emulate when alone is altitude callouts. For light airplanes, which climb and descend more slowly than jets, it is good practice to at least call out 500 and 100 feet before reaching a new altitude. On final, it is good to call, or at least think of, airspeed and sink rate.

On this trip I missed almost all the callouts. In no case did I "bust" an altitude but if the reminders are not there, eventually you will bust one. Lacking an altitude alert system in my airplane, I do always write down a new assigned altitude. Among other things, this convinces you that the controllers assign a lot of altitudes. On a leg from Mansfield, Ohio, to Trenton, N.J., I was assigned every altitude between 3,000 and 13,000 except 6,000, 11,000 and 12,000. That certainly defines a lot

of potential errors and it is worth writing down each
assignment.

Another miss was in setting the tower frequency in advance, ready for the simple flip-flop button when the frequency change was given. And this came on one of those approaches that illustrates how every approach should be treated as one to minimums. It was at Johnson County Industrial Airport in Kansas. The forecast was for 2,000 overcast but as I neared the area the weather was given to me as 500 broken, 2,000 overcast, and four miles visibility. On approaches, it is best to consider any clouds as overcast because even a piece of scattered cloud in the proper place can preclude a sighting of the approach lights or runway until the last moment.

That morning, I was following the procedure of talking myself through the approach. The turn on to final was close to the marker, which was okay because I had the area navigation system in the airplane set on the marker and knew exactly how far away it was, my proximity to the localizer, and the intercept angle. No surprises. The intercept was okay and the glideslope and localizer tracking got off to a good start. Then the approach controller told me to call the tower on the appropriate frequency. It wasn't preset so I had to divert a bit of attention from the flying to setting the radio and in the process I got about a dot off on both the localizer and glideslope. Minor, and no great factor, but something that could have been avoided had I thought through all factors for the approach in advance. It certainly kept this from qualifying as a perfect approach.

The day of that approach was a good one to fly because the weather was inclement all the way from Wichita, Kansas, where I started, to Trenton, where I was going. There were a lot of thunderstorms to the

152   south but my path was clear of everything but clouds and some bumpy rainshowers. It was still one of those days when you have to work a little harder than on a clear day.

After Industrial the next stop was to be Ohio State University airport at Columbus, Ohio. That's a reliever for Port Columbus and is usually a good fuel stop. But this day it wasn't to work that way. The radar at Columbus Approach Control shot craps, and as a result the center controller had to start reading off holding instructions to everyone. When she got to me I told her that I would just divert to Mansfield, Ohio, and she came right back with a clearance direct to there. It was only 64 miles away when I tuned up the Vortac, and a look at the chart revealed that I had complicated a lot of things by choosing Mansfield. Columbus was to be a handoff from Indianapolis Center to Columbus Approach Control. Going to Mansfield, I would be flying into Cleveland Center's area, then to Mansfield Approach Control. This meant coordination for the controllers who were already busy sorting out the mess caused by the radar outage.

The result was that I got within 25 miles of Mansfield at 13,000 feet, was at 9,000 when 12 miles from the airport, and had to do a dive-bomber approach. I do have a procedure for those—gear down, approach flaps, normal approach power, and 150 knots indicated will get rid of a lot of altitude fast, but somewhere in there I have to be satisfied that the last part of the approach will fit into one of the normal approach procedures that I use. We do have to try to fit our airplanes into the system as it operates, but if ever the occasion arises that they ask for something that seems like it will cause a problem, we have to be equally ready to tell the con-

troller that what they are asking for isn't possible in this   **153**
airplane with this pilot at this moment.

COMMUNICATING

The method in which we communicate is also part of a
perfect flight. And while there are as many communications procedures as there are pilots, one factor is the
determinant of success: Is the message clear and without excess verbiage? In busy areas, frequency time is a
limiting factor on the amount of traffic that can be handled and a pilot who makes a long-winded speech can
actually reduce the capacity of the air traffic control
system.

On this trip I gave myself one gig on communications. It came when the center controller handed me off
to another controller in the same center. I called him,
and he didn't answer. So I called again, and he didn't
answer. The proper procedure would have been to wait
a few moments; instead I switched back to the previous
controller. He rather curtly told me that the other controller was probably on a landline and couldn't answer
immediately, to wait a moment and call him again. I
should have known that and should have been a bit
more patient. As it was, I made my contribution to excess verbiage and flew on.

NITPICKING?

A lot of this might seem to be nitpicking, and it might
be. Maybe you can fly flights with the altitude wander-
ing all over the place, with the airspeed only within ten
or 20 knots of where it should be, and with a stitching
pattern along the airway or plotted route as the heading

154 wanders around. But flying should be a precise business because it is through precision that we manage the risks, which are very real. Flying is not simple, it is complicated—far more complicated than the rules would lead anyone to believe. But in its complexity, it is an activity that rewards individual effort far more than any other.

Whether your chosen activity is flying aerobatics, flying IFR, flying around, or just shooting landings, it is important to want to make every flight a perfect flight. They won't all be, rest assured, because there isn't a perfect pilot among us. But trying to make all flights perfect will help to minimize risks. It's very satisfying, too.

7

You, and You Alone

WHETHER YOU ARE the captain of an airliner, or a person who uses an airplane for transportation or recreation, you know that when flying you are doing something that depends largely on you, you alone. There will be times when you will be flying and wishing you are on the ground, the reverse of what is usually true, and when such occurs it has to come with the realization that for the wish to come true, you have to perform. There is no way a genie is going to slip into the left seat and do the flying and thinking for you. When you apply the power for takeoff, track down the centerline, and then fly the airplane off the runway, you have committed yourself to flying the rest of the flight, bringing the airplane back to the ground, and parking it.

An ocean sailor can be picked up by another ship; a skier can be rescued by a Saint Bernard with a jug of brandy, or a helicopter; a race driver can let off the gas and stop at any time; but when a pilot takes off, there is no midair rescue available, no way to successfully   155

156   stop except on a runway somewhere. Where airline
pilots have dispatch services, crews, and Part 121 rules
that minimize risks to the maximum extent possible,
general aviation pilots are pretty much on their own.
Perhaps this is one of the things that draws people to
flying. It is, when you think about it, not only a wonderful way to travel or amuse yourself. It is also a great
challenge. But you have to know something about yourself and your ability if you are to fly well.

REPENT

One pretty day I was in the back yard, puttering around,
when an airplane flew low over the area, buzzing. The
pilot kept it up and I got the number off the side of the
airplane. On a hunch, I called the FBO who handles the
flying program for a local college. Yes, it was one of
their airplanes. Yes, one of the college students was
flying it. I explained what had happened and suggested
that I would turn the pilot in to the FAA. When our
daughter got home from her classes at the college that
afternoon, she said she knew the pilot of the buzzing
airplane and that he wanted to come by and talk about
the incident. Sure, I said.

The young man was repentant indeed. I thought he
was going to break out in tears at one point in our
conversation, when I probed to see if he knew how
stupid and dangerous it was to fly low over congested
areas—to say nothing of the fact that it was illegal. I
asked him if he knew that aviation has a problem with
public relations, and that such exhibitionism in airplanes only drives another nail in the coffin, placing in
jeopardy the privileges of flight of other pilots. What
was he thinking about when he did this thoughtless and
stupid thing? He said he just didn't know.

In the end, I let him go, on the premise that it was   **157**
his youthful exuberance that led to the buzz job, not
some basic flaw in his personality that would lead to
further dangerous flying. But I later wondered if I had
done him any favor. Perhaps it would have been best to
report him to the FAA and suggest that they throw the
book at him. I didn't keep up with him. Maybe he has
come to an untimely end in an airplane but perhaps he
finished training for all his certificates and ratings and
is today flying as captain for a major airline. I hope the
latter is the case.

FEAR OR FEARLESS

Some pilots are a little fearful of flying, a lot of nonpilots
are scared out of their wits about airplanes, and some
pilots and nonpilots seem to have no fear at all of airplanes. The best balance comes somewhere in between.

Flying might best be considered as similar to bull-
fighting, where you know that the bull would like nothing better than to do you in. The airplane, fond as you
might be of it, has to be viewed in an adversarial role.
It stands ready to kill you if you don't perform. That's
true of cars and boats and a lot of other things but not
to the extent that it is true of airplanes. You can fly the
airplane into things, such as thunderstorms, that might
exceed your and its ability to survive. You can get ice
on the airplane and render it unflyable. If you lose control of the airplane, it can be, along with you, on the
ground and shattered in a very short time. If you do
something so simple as forgetting to properly drain the
sumps, or putting the fuel selector on the correct position, the engine might fail at a bad time on takeoff and
leave you between a rock and a hard place. Maybe
when you open the hangar door, you should look at it

158 and say, "Well, partner, what are you going to do to try to kill me today?" Of course the airplane doesn't do it. You do it to yourself. But the best attitude is that the airplane can be deadly if you don't do all the right things with it. The accident investigators make much of human failure. It is very real. And you and I are susceptible to it.

Is that an overly negative attitude? I don't think so. It is really positive because it is realistic. And when people who aren't pilots fly with me, I try to help them understand that in personally operated vehicles the risk can increase as the square of the speed—unless you take into account that the speed is doubled or tripled over a car and a third dimension is added. Make all the necessary allowances for this and the risks can be managed.

This doesn't mean that you should be afraid of airplanes. Just respectful. I'm certainly not scared of them, but like anyone who has flown for a time, I've had uneasy moments in airplanes. And I try never to be complacent. A person who is afraid of flying is uneasy all the time, whether or not there is an unusual threat out there. Acrophobia, a fear of height, could have something to do with this. Also, to some people the sensations of flight might be unsettling. Even light G loads are upsetting, and as much as you explain turbulence it still bothers some. If a person wants to learn to fly but can't get over basic fear, there is no question that the person should forget it. Flying in the face of a basic fear proves nothing, and a person who persists in becoming a pilot despite this fear proves nothing.

That isn't to say that even for the coolest pilots there aren't moments when the adrenalin flows faster than others. One of the times that I find most challenging is when we are taking air-to-air photographs for our magazine. Flying two airplanes, usually dissimilar airplanes, in relatively close formation requires total concentration and, as many times as I have done it, the first join-up on each flight, or the formation takeoff, always gets the juices flowing. I know that there is more risk in this type of flying than in most anything else I do in an airplane and while I take every extra possible effort to minimize the risk on every photo mission, some always lurks in the background.

We were photographing a Beech 1900, using a Piper T-tail Lance as a photo platform. These flights are flown within a couple of hours of sunrise or sunset for best lighting on the subject airplane. This was a morning flight on one of the prettiest mornings I have ever seen. The sky was clear and there was an early morning mist in the fields. The Lance pilot had been instructed to climb at maximum continuous power and 120 knots indicated airspeed. I would leave takeoff flaps extended in the 1900 for climb, to have a better margin between indicated airspeed and stalling speed.

A formation takeoff isn't a good idea in two airplanes of such different performance so I spotted the Lance the length of the runway and then charged off after it. The best way to join is like the military does it with tankers. Approach the photo airplane lower than its altitude. Then dissipate the extra speed by pulling up to it. It is a very precise business and I have seen people with extensive formation practice in years past forget

160 how to do it, or be unable to do it with airplanes that
are somewhat less than fully compatible.

There is a very intense feeling as you close on the
other airplane. If my hair could stand up, it probably
would. But once you settle in and make peace with the
dynamics of, in this case, a larger airplane and a much
smaller airplane, the intensity settles down. But to the
very end of a photo mission, the peak of alertness has
to remain. The photographer wants you to move the
airplane around, per his hand signals, and each change
in position requires another study of the dynamics. If he
wants a bit more bank in the turns, that requires a
power change and, indeed, the power has to be juggled
on a continuous basis. I have come to greatly dislike
vernier throttles because of photo missions. That's hard
work, flying one with a vernier.

Strong Reminder

Flying these missions is, to me, a good reminder of how
totally involved the individual has to be in managing
risks. There's nothing between you and a blazing collision other than your brain, eyes, hands, and feet. The
time it would take to render both airplanes unflyable
would be less than a second. And everything has to be
considered. For example, when flying a larger airplane
with a smaller one, and making circles as photogra-
phers like to do, it's best to climb a little all the time lest
you fly back into the wake turbulence. That is very
disconcerting in close formation. So is a surprise from
other traffic. And it is only the realization that this flying
tolerates nothing short of a flawless performance that
keeps the risk down. One of our fine *Flying* readers
wrote and asked why the pilot in the subject airplane
was always looking at the camera. Vain? Not really,

and if you ever see one looking somewhere else, you
know that was a risky operation.

One of our staffers suggested that we do an article on formation flying. I couldn't bring myself to do this, though. To do a story on it might prompt some people to go out and try it. And the risks here are, honestly, not as easy to manage as some of the others. I have, when flying with military pilots, very much admired both the precision with which they fly formation and their ability to teach it to other pilots. But they do it mostly in like airplanes, and that does make a difference—especially if there is any turbulence. Even then, it requires total concentration as well as a cool hand on the stick and throttle. So it has seemed advisable to leave this as a total "don't."

TALK TO YOURSELF

The ability to honestly communicate with yourself is an important part of the flying equation. Take, for example, a landing on a smaller airport than you normally use. If you quietly review every factor in advance, and level with yourself about your ability to do this, the chances of success are much better.

One place where I always give myself a good talking to is at Sugarbush, in Vermont. The fact that the locals call the airport the S.S. Sugarbush might give you some idea of the nature of the strip. It isn't overly short at 2,575 feet but it is in the mountains and the runway peaks in the middle, meaning that you had best get the landing and most of the stopping done before you reach the middle and start downhill.

The lecture on the arrival procedure starts with the business about the horizon being at the base of the hills, better managed with the airplane's attitude indicator

162   than the seat of your pants. Then comes the part about precise airspeed maintenance. The short field arrival procedure calls for a 72-knot approach speed. At that, the Sugarbush runway barely fits the minimum runway length that I use. The airline Part 121 requirement is that the performance charts must show that you can be 50 feet high over the threshold and then land and stop in 60 percent of the runway. I use that to have the same margin that airline passengers enjoy. So the lecture is that success is based solely on my ability to fly a 72-knot approach to the runway, crossing the threshold at 50 feet or less. Do it any other way and the margins go away. And if I can't convince myself to do it that way, the only thing to do is fly to a larger airport and rent a car.

COMPLACENCY

When a pilot becomes complacent about flying, it is apparently because sight is lost of the fact that the airplane can get you if the old guard is let down. More has been made of this recently because of the level of automation that is finding its way into cockpits. Airliners have been automated to the point that one crewmember, the flight engineer, has been eliminated. And on a routine flight, the two crewmembers have less to do than the three did previously. Warning systems abound. Even on simple general aviation airplanes we have done a lot in navigation, largely with loran C, which in most of the U.S. gives the same navigational ability that the large airplanes have with their sophisticated systems. Autopilots are the norm rather than the exception in airplanes used for travel. Talking checklists have made an appearance, and on at least one new aircraft engine (the Porsche) the control of the propeller

pitch and mixture are automated. And we are likely to   **163**
see more rather than less of that.

This is all to the good, because the technology in
electronics has moved forward so much in recent times
where aerodynamics and propulsion technology appears to have reached a bit of a peak. Compare Concorde and its cockpit, avionics, and systems to a Boeing
767. While Concorde is stunning in an aerodynamic
sense, its cockpit looks old-fashioned. Mechanical instruments and a flight engineer's panel that is overwhelming are located in the pointed end of Concorde.
The 767 is both clean in design and simple in appearance by comparison. The Boeing also has more extensive warning systems and is certified to land with lower
visibility. But does this make one airplane safer than
the other? I think not. Personally, I'll always bet more
on the ability of the pilot flying the airplane than on the
automated capability of the machine. There is always
the possibility that pilots flying the more automated
airplane might become complacent. I know some of the
pilots who fly Concorde for British Airways and, believe me, the ones I know are not complacent about
flying the airplane. And I am not saying that 767 pilots
are, just that they would have to develop a better guard
against this in their airplane, where there is less to do.

There has been a case of one of the new automated
jet airliners running out of fuel because of a miscalcula-
tion in adding fuel to the tanks for the flight. All the
automation did not keep the captain of this aircraft from
having to execute a dead stick landing in a widebody.
And it was widely held that the pilot's off-duty glider
flying activity was a definite benefit as he flew the big
airplane to a successful landing. In another incident, the
crew of a widebody sat and watched all their electronic
flight instrument system screens go blank. The glass

164 cockpit failed, leaving them with the small mechanical instruments to use in landing the aircraft. Fortunately the weather was clear. How would they have done in an approach to minimums? Who knows? It would probably depend as much on the pilot's background as anything else. If the pilot were to be a computer nerd, dependent on such things, it might be one thing. If the pilot were to be a true airman, it might be another thing indeed.

MANAGER OF THE DIALS

Can a pilot maintain peak alertness when the role is relegated to one of being a manager? This might be where we'd see a split between the older and younger pilots. The theory would be that the younger folks are more in tune with automation and electronic solutions and can spend alert hours watching the machines fly and navigate themselves—even land themselves in the case of Category 3 (very low-visibility) landings.

But somewhere down the line, say after watching hundreds of perfect Category 3 landings, would the guard go down, maybe just a little bit? Or if you develop confidence in the low-altitude alert and autothrottles system on the airplane, might there not be a tendency to assume that the airplane can manage itself quite well if only you put the correct numbers in the windows and that it would warn you of excessive sink rate and proximity to terrain? And might the rote insertion of numbers into a machine time and time again lead next to less attention to putting in the correct numbers? To me, it doesn't bode well if we think of ourselves as managers of electronics equipment instead of as pilots. No matter how fancy the machine, there is some combination of factors that could lead you back to the dark ages,

where thinking and flying skills, not electronics, might   **165**
be required to get the airplane on the ground safely.

SIMULATORS

The airlines use simulators extensively, as do business
jet crews. And these are invaluable because it is possible to simulate failures in a way that would be dangerous in an airplane. You can simulate all the way to an
unflyable condition and still have everyone survive.
The biggest mistake a pilot might make in simulator
flying would be to develop the idea that these things can
only happen in the simulator. That is not true. They can
happen in the airplane as well and once you look at the
seamy side of things in the simulator, then you can think
about how, in the airplane, you can prevent events from
progressing to the point where control was lost and the
simulator crashed.

AUTOPILOT

The automated device that most of us are exposed to on
a regular basis is the autopilot and it pays to have a
careful relationship with this as well as a full understanding of your perception of the autopilot.

I was flying with a pilot one half-scuzzy day and
noticed that he hand flew the airplane when it was clear
of clouds but would turn the autopilot on before he flew
into clouds. His explanation was the the autopilot could
fly the airplane better than he could fly it, so why not?
This is the same explanation pilots give for letting autopilots fly all the low approaches. The autopilot can do
as good if not a better job of flying a low approach, so
why not let it fly and let the pilot be a monitor? That
way there is some redundancy. A pilot might catch a

166 developing error in an autopilot's performance, where if you are hand flying, the autopilot has no chance of catching your mistakes.

There is some validity to looking at autopilots in this manner but it has to be done very carefully, lest the pilot become rusty, or complacent, or, worse, a combination of both. I know pilots who I feel have a blind faith in electronic and mechanical solutions, and I hope the faith never betrays them. If the glass cockpit goes blank, or the power fails completely, there is no question that the pilot has to be ready to go back to the basics.

THE TIMES

Again, my feeling about these things is probably a product of what was going on when I started flying instruments, in 1955. Sophisticated autopilots were all but unheard of—the first one I had was a wing-leveler that used the rudder only. There was no radar information available from air traffic control and certainly there was no on-board gear to use for thunderstorm avoidance. You were on your own. Navigation was with an ADF and VOR, and still with some low-frequency ranges. The radar system wasn't in place so separation was all based on timing and the pilot's navigation. There was no DME yet. Even glideslopes were almost unheard of in light airplanes. A localizer approach was about as good as it got.

Given all those factors, a lot more time was put into navigating than today. We had to know where we were and how fast we were going. The allowable miss was three minutes either side of an estimated time over a point. Separation was based on our hitting these estimates within three minutes or calling with a revised

estimate. The system that was based on this had very
little capacity and because there were so few airplanes
out there flying IFR, they had a large margin. Which is
to say that having not many airplanes in a large sky
helps.

The question that I ask myself about navigation is
whether or not I have become complacent about it because of electronics. With a Northstar M-1 loran that
works beautifully plus a King KNS 81 navigational system and a backup VOR system, plus dual glideslopes
and dual transponders and encoders, and the old faithful ADF, and radar and a Stormscope, am I prone to let
the microchips do the thinking and go along for a mind-
less ride? I guess that is possible but I do work at maxi-
mizing the use of the equipment and still work at
keeping up with track and position on the chart. I like
to know the airplane's position in relation to terrain and
airports because you never know when the need to
know might become critical.

KEY FACTOR

In any self-examination there is one factor that comes
up that, to me, is not aptly named. It is what is referred
to as "judgment." The reason that I don't particularly
like the word is because I have to get to definition 3 in
The Random House Dictionary of the English Language
to find what I think it means. The proper definition: "the
ability to judge, make a decision, or form an opinion
objectively, authoritatively, and wisely, esp. in matters
affecting action; good sense; discretion; a man of sound
judgment." The reason I like that definition is that it is
held by some that you can't teach judgment, and that
even though most airplane wrecks are a product of poor
judgment, no amount of increased training would help.

168   But doesn't training help you learn to make good decisions and to form opinions objectively, authoritatively,
and wisely?

One key to this is probably in learning to make
decisions, and in flying this action is best based on
procedures and standards that are thought through in
advance. The decision has to always be biased in the
safe and conservative direction.

I was flying along in a light twin one day and noticed that the left fuel tank was farther down than the
right. Turning the autopilot off showed that the airplane
was right-wing heavy. I had watched them fill the airplane and both tanks had been filled equally. The cap
was in view and no fuel was siphoning. I looked aft and
there was a vapor trail behind the left engine. Fuel.
What to do? Secure the engine and land at the nearest
suitable airport. That's a simple matter of landing to
investigate anything that is unusual. To fly on would, to
me, be inviting more problems than might already be
present.

The place where poor judgment is most often cited
as being a problem for people traveling in airplanes
relates to weather. The big items are continuing VFR
into adverse weather conditions, and descending into
the ground on instrument (usually nonprecision) approaches. And these are things that pilots can be taught
not to do in a good training program, with reinforcement
in recurrent training.

BAD OLD DAYS

Almost all pilots engaged in at least some form of scud
running in the '50s and into the '60s, as light-airplane
IFR began to take hold as an alternative. A project that
Russell Munson and I did for *Flying* in the '70s re-

minded me how tenuous this form of flying really is.

The project was a photo series that would show how deteriorating weather conditions look from the cockpit. To do it effectively, we had to fly in deteriorating weather conditions. I lived in Little Rock and the FAA's Southwest Region, under the directorship of Henry Newman, was very helpful as we did this. The deal was that I would keep them posted on where we would be flying and when; they would in turn block the minimum en route altitude over the area. Then if our scud running reached the point where it would no longer work, we could, with FAA's blessing, pull up to the MEA and give them a call; they would then clear us back to Little Rock for the ILS and we could start out again. I took advantage of that arrangement a couple of times during the flying, which was in a Cessna 172, and the thing that was most impressive to me is that I was following all the techniques of an experienced scud runner and was surprised when I lost ground contact. Clearly, if good "judgment" is to prevail a pilot has to be trained to make an early decision regarding not continuing VFR into adverse weather conditions.

LONELY BUSINESS

In that early instrument flying, where you did more flying than talking (as no longer seems to be the case today) a pilot could become rather lonely. Droning through the clouds, not sure there was no storm up ahead, gave what might best be described as an interesting feeling. Alone, this is all up to you. No help from anywhere, very little information from anywhere. That feeling was almost continuous then.

Now, with all the electronics, better information from the ground, and with people talking so much on the

170   radio that we might need another category of flight—Vocal Flight Rules—there are seldom times when you seem so alone. I used to fly back and forth from Little Rock to Wichita a lot in my Cherokee Six, Skylane, or Skyhawk, and quickly learned that this area is a hotbed of convective activity. The lonely times would come when there was weather out there and I would take all the available information and head for the best-looking spot. With the decision made, when the depth charges started going off the feeling was one of being in this rainy and bumpy cloud alone. That man on the ground couldn't help, nobody could. My deal: fly out of it. And, in retrospect, if we have any problem with complacency, or with our individual relationship to flying and the attendant responsibilities, it might be because of electronics and people to talk to on the ground on a continuous basis if we choose. The fact is, we are as alone in being the total master of the fate of the flight as ever. It just might not seem that way.

8

Airports

A S PILOTS we think most of all about airplanes, those wonderful things that fly. But the air itself and the airports that we use play an equally important role. In the good old days even people who didn't fly shared our fascination with airports. When I was a kid, LaGuardia in New York had an observation deck, as did many other airports around the country. You could go there and watch airplanes; with a nickle (or was it a penny?) you could get some time on binoculars to watch the airplanes come and go on a more intimate basis.

Airports have since come to show that they are profit centers, ringed with chain-link fences and security. It costs more to park for a day than some airline tickets used to cost. But some airports still have a soul beneath all the latter-day hype. At Washington National, for example, the core of the terminal is the same building that I went through as a kid, in 1943, on my first airline trip. And I will always have a strong feeling for

171

172   some airports, because they are nice places or spur pleasant memories.

WASHINGTON NATIONAL

I have always thought of Washington National as our nation's airport of record. The terminal was a classic to begin with and while today it bears the scars of expansion and the evolution of the airlines from DC-3s to jets, the airport still exists on a relatively small bit of ground with a basic terminal. The words "Washington National Airport" are in gold on the front of the building, perhaps so that pilots and passengers alike will have no doubt about where they have landed.

It wasn't designed to be a jetport and it isn't a jetport. To watch large airplanes fly from the relatively short runways is almost to see gravity defied. Yet it is done day after day, with few incidents over the history of the airport. This is a tribute to what pilots can do when challenged. One airline pilot told me that he approached National with a feeling different from that he had when approaching any other airport. Sit up and pay attention. It is different. Landing south, it's a visual approach down the river with a turn onto a very short final right at the last. There is an ILS to the north. The three runways cross about in the middle so the controllers have to "shoot the gap," as they call it. The primary runway is the north-south; they work traffic on and off the other two runways between the takeoffs and landings on the primary.

National isn't a place for the faint of heart. The very high rate of use, up to 130 VFR operations per hour and 60 IFR operations per hour, means that everyone has to do it correctly. If a pilot can't adapt to the hectic nature of the place then the pilot should go elsewhere. Lore has

it that one general aviation pilot became so flustered by
the fast pace that he landed in the Potomac River in
total confusion.

Despite all this, there is overwhelming logic to the
way they run National. The controllers know the airport, they know the pilots, and they know the airplanes.
It is no trick for them to play the airspace to the maximum, using the Anacostia and Potomac rivers as fly-
ways to thread airplanes between the restricted
airspace that protects the White House, the Capitol,
and the national monuments, and to separate them from
airplanes flying at Andrews Air Force Base and Dulles
International Airport. The primary flow of traffic con-
sists of narrow-body airline jets (widebodys not allowed) using the north-south runway. Occasionally
airline jets will use Runway 33, but I have never seen
one use 15, 3, or 21. And when they are offered 33, many
captains refuse because there is but 5,189 feet of pave-
ment available and it is a close-in circling approach.
When they do accept, you can all but hear the crew say
"whoa" as the airplane roars to a stop, reverse blasting
and brakes smoking.

With the primary flow on the longest runway, they
can use the other two runways for commuter airliners
and general aviation airplanes. If it is a south operation,
they use 21 and 15; on a north operation it's 3 and 33.
They prefer to use 21 and 33 for landings and 3 and 15
for takeoffs for a simple reason: You can taxi to 3 and
15 without crossing the primary runway and crossing
while taxiing uses as much airport capacity as does
crossing while taking off or landing. Also, for northeast-
bound aircraft, a turn up the Anacostia River right after
takeoff gets the slower airplane out of the way quickly.
Airline jets do not use the Anacostia corridor because
there's no room for them to maneuver to or from the

174   primary runway. On windy days, when traffic is backed up, if you'll take runway 3 (with the wind from 300 at 30 knots, for example), they'll get you right out. But it is up to you to decide that you can safely handle that much crosswind.

Rampside

If the air traffic is hectic at the airport, the ramp traffic is equally brisk. Interesting, too. Corporate jets swarm the Butler Aviation FBO operation and you hardly ever pass through the place without seeing a celebrity of some note. Strange sights, too. I'll never forget the evening I flew there to attend the Collier Trophy dinner. I am not a tuxedo person but one was required for this occasion. I borrowed it from the kids next door, who are, because of age, tapered in a different direction than I. And because I was just going for the evening, I had to fly in the tux. I felt like a fool walking through the Butler lobby looking like an overstuffed penguin, but I wasn't the only one. Arnold Palmer had arrived a few minutes earlier, having flown down from a golf tournament in Philadelphia, but he had an advantage: someone else flew his Citation 3 and he changed into his tux en route.

It's a democratic place, too. When all the parking places are full at the FBO, all airplanes are shunted off to the south 40, where a van will eventually come for you. Matters not whether the airplane is a Cessna 172 or a Gulfstream IV; if the lot is full you go south. Some pilots feel that the personnel at the FBO are a bit brusque, but they have to be that way. Theirs is a limited resource; as with the airspace, it only works if everyone knows how to fit their piece into the puzzle.

If you use National well, it is with a satisfaction

that you fit into the fast lane without a ripple. If a pilot   175
doesn't find that satisfaction, there are other airports in
the area.

In three-dozen years or more of flying I have landed
on a few short of 700 airports. National is my favorite.
It is every man's link to the seat of government. Land,
walk to the subway or to a cab, and in 15 minutes you
can be face-to-face with the bureaucrat of choice. It is
true that you do have to have a reservation to go there
IFR, but anyone who plans ahead has little trouble with
this rule. And when I think back to the days before the
reservation rule, and the chaos that would often result
when everyone was trying to get to National at the
same time, it is easy to smile on the IFR reservation
system. In fact, just for fun, I made a reservation to
arrive there in the first hour of the first day of the rule.
The FAA administrator was at the airport that morning,
and reportedly asked a tower operator if that single-
engine Cessna had complied with the rule.

SMALLER PONDS

The purpose of any airport is to be a link with the rest
of the world. They are like highways or rivers, open for
use by anyone. In the congested areas of the country,
airports have trouble finding space because they tend to
benefit a smaller percentage of the population. With
freeways, trains, and subways, and millions of people,
the interest in airports is less than in an area where the
nearest big city is hundreds of miles away. And that is
why the per capita ownership of airplanes in the U.S.
increases rapidly as you go west. It is also why airports
are more appealing in more remote areas.

My old friend Jim Gaston has a resort on the White
River in Arkansas. The front lawn was for years a 2,200-

176 foot-long grass runway. (It has since been extended.) Another friend of mine, Dr. Dale Briggs from Little Rock, is a fan of the White River area and spent many hours driving back and forth on his time off. Then one day I flew Dale up to Gaston's in my Skyhawk, for lunch. It took 45 minutes to fly the trip and he was impressed. I think he almost thought about learning how to fly, even though I don't think he really liked airplanes. But the ability to connect places like that, on a personal basis, was appealing.

It was during the time I lived in Arkansas in the '70s, too, that I learned how proud people can be of airports. I served for several years on the Arkansas Aeronautics Commission, one year as chairman, and our primary purpose was to use the sales tax collected on all aviation-related sales for airport and navaid development. It was a low-budget operation with two paid folks. The director was Eddie Holland; he had an assistant, and a gaggle of unpaid commissioners. At that time our maximum grant was $10,000. Not a lot of money, but airports could get more than one grant, spaced by a year. One shot would buy an NDB; somehow we stretched it to help one airport get a localizer, and some airport managers would take the ten grand and use it to buy raw materials that would be used with county or city equipment, on donated land, to build an airport. The reward for our labor as commissioners came when it was time to deliver the money to the community. No checks in the mail. Nothing would do but we go to the town for a delivery ceremony. I have pictures in my file of the county judge, mayor, sheriff, or whoever was in charge, accepting the airport grant check. Eddie Holland had a clipping service, and the aid to airports got a lot of press. There were luncheons, speeches, and ribbon cuttings. Those folks were proud of their air-

ports. They were a link to the rest of the world. Small
airports, yes, but very useful.

BEST OF THE REST

If National is picked as a favorite airport, what is second best? I guess the airport that I have used more than any other, Mercer County at Trenton, N.J., has to fill that bill. It has no particular claim to fame. Air Force One did land there once, with President Reagan on board, and numerous lesser functionaries have come to town through the airport. It has had large airline service a few times, but not to the extent that it attracted enough passengers for the service to be viable. A few large corporations built hangars there but the location, halfway between New York and Philadelphia, was close to the big action but apparently not close enough. In fact, the airport seems to have changed little from 1959, when I first moved there, to the present time. If there was a head count, I doubt that there are a lot more based airplanes now than then. The primary airport improvements have been an ILS and the lengthening of runway 6/24. There is actually less hangar space available to the public now because one big World War II hangar burned and the other was torn down to be replaced by modern but smaller structures.

The only lore relates to the tower. Because the approach end of the ILS runway is down in a hole, when you are at the 200 feet above touchdown zone decision height you are but 115 feet above the top of the relatively low-slung control tower. And, you guessed it, one grungy day the tower folks came eyeball to eyeball with a pilot who was trying to get his act straight on a missed approach. So they painted the tower in a checkerboard, red-and-white pattern that was quite ugly but also quite

178   visible. I don't know how long it stayed painted that
way, but recently they painted it back a nice camou-
flage gray. Apparently the memory of that near-colli-
sion has faded.

WEATHER

When you fly from the same airport for a long time, a
feeling develops for the peculiarities of the area
weather. The Delaware River runs to the west of Trenton, only a couple of miles away. A lot of airports are
close to rivers, fog forms along rivers, and at Trenton
the low spot at the approach end of the ILS runway is
closer in elevation to the river than is the center of the
airport. There's no runway visual range equipment on
the airport, so the visibility minimum is set by what the
tower can see. But often they can see a half mile when,
on the approach, you are firmly locked in fog at the
decision height. When Trenton reports 200 and a half,
don't bet on it. Also on the ILS, someone has been
feeding the trees on short final and it is only a matter
of time until one dot low will scare the birds out of their
nests.
        Trenton's other personality traits relate to wind.
Because there are low hills to the northwest, there are
world-class bumps around the airport when the wind
howls from the northwest. And there is usually a sinking spell on final to Runway 34.

BACK COURSE

Another airport I always liked is Adams Field, or Little
Rock Regional Airport, in Arkansas. I used to instruct
there, in radioless Taylorcrafts, using light signals from
the tower, landing and taking off in the grass infield.

This caused no problem to the air carrier traffic. But it 179
was when instrument flying started that Little Rock became more interesting. It is in a part of the country
noted for petulant weather and a combination of fog, a
steam generating plant, and a back-course approach
used to bedevil pilots. This particular approach was to
Runway 22; the steam plant was perhaps a mile from
the end of the runway. When the airport would have the
required mile visibility for a back-course approach, the
steam would rise and restrict visibility on the final approach course. If you were flying at the minimum descent altitude, when you emerged from the restricted
visibility caused by the steam, you might well be too
high to make a normal landing unless flying a light airplane. That resulted in a lot of missed approaches and
to the eventual installation of an ILS on that runway.

HOMEPORTS

Three airports—Beech Field, Cessna Field, and Lock
Haven as they were popularly called—are where the
majority of the airplanes flying in the U.S. today made
their first flight. Each of those fields has, or had, a personality.

Beech Field

Beech Field is where Beech Aircraft Corporation has
been since the beginning, right after the Great Depression. The original factory buildings are buried in the
present sprawling complex. Until Raytheon bought the
company in 1980, things changed very slowly at Beech.
The property is a section of land, one square mile, so the
runway is a mile long. For years there were wires across
the north end but these were removed after Raytheon

180   executives started flying jets into the airport. A big hangar at the northwest end of the runway and a plant at the southwest end make crosswinds quite interesting. The instrument approaches to the airport are challenging. There are straight-in area navigation approaches to the north-south runway but the usual approach is a VOR, circling approach. Trouble is, in Wichita the weather is usually either pretty good or very low, at least low for a circling approach. The result is that a lot of folks wind up at the municipal airport, where there is an ILS.

Beech is close to McConnell Air Force Base and VFR procedures call for a low-level approach, to stay below the McConnell traffic. But nothing like at Cessna Field.

Cessna Field

Like Beech Field, and most other airports in the Great Plains, Cessna Field has a north-south runway. It is different in the sense that it is adjacent to McConnell Air Force Base. How did thousands of Cessna airplanes successfully come and go beneath the pattern that is full of military jets? Quite well, although the arrival and departure was somewhat different. The traffic pattern altitude for Cessna was (the airport is now closed) 300 feet above the ground or lower. Never higher. On an instrument approach it was always amazing that you had to go lower from the minimum descent altitude to enter the traffic pattern. It had to be a close pattern, too, because Beech was a short distance to the north and McConnell adjacent to the south. The pattern was flown as much using landmarks as anything else. A road defined the line between Beech's air and Cessna's air for

a south landing or a north takeoff. Going the other way,   **181**
McConnell didn't like it if you flew over the hospital
making a lot of noise so the corner of a base housing
project was used to define the flight path.

I landed there many times, the first in 1953 in a
Piper Super Cruiser to attend the 50th anniversary cele-
bration of the Wrights' first flight and the introduction
of the Cessna 180. Flew away with three new airplanes,
too, a Skyhawk, a Cardinal RG, and a P210. It is with
some admitted wistfulness that I fly by there now and
remember the days when light airplanes came from the
plant across the field from the strip in large numbers.

Cessna had a parallel strip on the other side of the
field from the delivery center where production took
place and experimental flight tests were flown. It was
off this strip that the only serious incidents I am aware
of occurred. One pilot took off and collided with an F-4
right after takeoff; another ran afoul of a heavy jet's
wake turbulence.

The road into the delivery center was one of the
few in the world with a runway-closed X painted on it.
This was because one grungy day a pilot flying a 310
wrapped it around onto final to the narrow runway and
landed on the road instead. They decided that could
happen again, thus the X.

Lock Haven

The airport at Lock Haven, Pennsylvania, used to be
called "Cub Haven"; now it is the William T. Piper
Memorial Airport, in honor of the founder of Piper Aircraft Corporation. When he—called "Pop" by his ador-
ing family and "Mr. Piper" by the rest of us—was
running the place it reflected his spartan nature. Mr.

182   Piper would usually walk to work from his relatively modest home in Lock Haven. When he flew, it was in his Tri-Pacer and when the company brought out its first twin, the Apache, he wondered aloud if his dealers could really afford to stock and sell such luxury. Cub Haven is on the Susquehanna River, which flooded and brought misery to Piper and Lock Haven more than once. It is also surrounded by mountains. For years the downwind leg to land west (in Pennsylvania most runways run east-west) snuggled up to the mountain but with the advent of airplanes with higher approach speeds they changed to a right-hand pattern. At a speed over about 90 knots there simply wasn't room to turn final.

    Of the three home airports for most airplanes flying today, I felt the closest kinship to Lock Haven. I first went there as a little boy and Mr. Piper and his sons, Howard ("Pug"), Bill, Jr., and Tony, always made you feel like you were part of their family. When Mr. Piper passed away, my father and I flew through a snowstorm to get to his funeral. The weather cleared a bit during the service, and three Cubs flew low over the church, in tribute to the man who did as much in developing general aviation as anyone. I never discussed it with my father but am sure he felt as I did that an era passed into history along with Mr. Piper.

    The runway at Lock Haven is relatively short, 3,350 feet, and when taking off west it launches you out over town. To my knowledge, though, nobody ever had to find a place to land in town because of a power failure. And remember, the majority of the Piper airplanes flying first flew from Lock Haven although Vero Beach will exceed that at some point because Lock Haven has been closed for a while and Vero is their only location now.

The operating environment at Piper was always a **183** little more relaxed than at the other places. If they knew you, they were prone to toss you the keys to a new model and tell you to go fly it. If there were checkouts, they were brief. Because most Pipers flew a lot alike, this worked well enough but there were interesting moments.

One interesting time for me came as I was leaving Lock Haven with Twin Comanche N7001Y, the first production airplane, on May 17, 1963. When I turned the fuel pumps off after takeoff, the right engine quit. I turned the pumps back on but it didn't start back up right away so I feathered the prop and brought the airplane back in. They had another, N7004Y, fourth off the line, and I took it away for evaluation.

The other interesting time came in a Pressurized Navajo. This was a heavy airplane for a light twin, not overly blessed with power. The airplane was loaded with promotional material to go to the Reading Air Show and I was to fly it there with a pilot from Piper. As with airplanes that are new to me, I carefully went through the checklist, checking everything twice. Then I pulled out on the runway and applied maximum power to the big Lycoming engines. The airplane seemed to be accelerating rather poorly, and about 2,000 feet down the runway I asked the pilot in the right seat if it was moving out normally. He said something to the effect that he didn't know, he hadn't flown the airplane much. Charging on with the knowledge that Piper wouldn't build an airplane that wouldn't fly out of Lock Haven, I rotated near the end of the runway and pointed the nose of the airplane at the top of the tallest tree. If anything would work, that would. It did.

Carroll Cone Field

One other airport is held in fond memory because it was where I had my first airplane ride and later did some interesting flying. It is Carroll Cone Field (now closed) at Fordyce, Arkansas. My father was instrumental in having the airport there, for he was a Cub and Aeronca dealer after the Great Depression as well as running a flying school. J. Carroll Cone was a native of Arkansas who became the equivalent of today's FAA administrator. Whether the airport was ever officially named for him I know not. The airport never, to my knowledge, appeared on any chart and that was just as well. The most optimistic measurement of its runway length came to a whopping 1,400 feet.

I flew a lot of airplanes in and out of the little strip, including Twin Comanches, Comanches, and Bonanzas. It would tolerate only airplanes that could be brought across the fence at 65 or 70 knots and that had good brakes. Departures were only with enough fuel to fly 40 miles, with reserves, to a larger airport for tank topping. There were airplanes based there on a rather occasional basis. The landing to the northeast had the best approaches, though they weren't all that good. Landing south you had to clear houses and trees right across the street from the approach end of the runway. There was never any question that the runway length was marginal at best, but for years it was Fordyce's link to the rest of the world. To my knowledge, the town's most famous son, "Bear" Bryant, never used the little airport, although he did come home in the University of Alabama's airplane when a new and larger airport was built in the '60s.

There are a lot of other airports with personalities. Just mentioning a few isn't meant to slight the other ones. Asheville, North Carolina, with its perpetual awful weather and surrounding mountains; Farmington, New Mexico, on a mesa; Charleston, West Virginia, where they levelled a mountaintop to build the airport; Easton, Pennsylvania, which is owned by Eddie and Lib Braden at this writing and has been owned and operated by Eddie and Lib for over 50 years; and a lot more. But each person's feeling about certain airports is something to savor and cherish. There's something special about the ground off which we fly.

AIR

There's something special about the air, or the routes we fly, too. And while we might develop a familiarity with certain routes, the weather is always ready and willing to change the character and complexion of even the most familiar path. The routes that I have flown most, Little Rock–Wichita, New Jersey–Florida, and New Jersey–Wichita, all have a meaning. When I fly those, I have a feeling that I am going down a familiar path on which I have seen a lot of sights and had a lot of good and interesting experiences. All have been flown over 100 times, some a lot more than 100 times.

EN ROUTE WEATHER

The familiarity with the landmarks is one thing. Those routes could be flown on a clear day without a radio or a map after 100 trips. The fascinating thing about routes

186   is weather and the track that you fly has a lot to do with the weather that is encountered.

Take the air between Little Rock and Wichita: The bearing is about 300 degrees to Wichita and 120 to Little Rock. That is perpendicular to a typical cold front and parallel to a typical warm front. This is also an area where rapid low development along a stationary front is a frequent phenomenon. When flying the route, the challenge becomes one of getting a good idea about the synopsis. Is a mature low out there with clearly defined warm and cold fronts? Or is a low developing somewhere out there, your guess as good as mine on where, that will crank up and create fronts as the circulation around it matures? Also in relation to fronts, the Boston and Ouachita Mountains affect the southeastern half of the 300-nm route; they can serve to slow the progress of a front. A mountain range to the south of the route, while not high, can still dish up some strong up- and downdrafts and contribute to the development of convective activity.

Where clearly defined fronts were concerned, timing was important because with cold fronts, perhaps waiting a while would let the cold front go through and allow a calmer flight. With warm fronts, leaving earlier might keep the flight below the slope of the warm front while leaving later might give a better ride south of the warm front. The most important strategic decision related to a low that was becoming strong quickly or that was already strong. The area east and northeast of these was a bad place to be.

For the first few years that I flew this route, there were some mystifying times. A feel for the development of new low-pressure areas was lacking. Knowledge came slowly that if the wind was more southerly and stronger than forecast, something new was cranking up there. Also, if there was a stationary front, or a weather 187 map with two or three ill-defined lows to the west, the stronger and more southerly wind meant that one of the lows had become primary and was making a move. When this was encountered, it was time to set off on a new quest for weather information because what was gathered before takeoff was no longer likely valid.

Tornado Alley

A lot of different places in the country are called tornado alley, and between Little Rock and Fort Smith should be one of them. A photo mission in my Skyhawk gave an example of how capricious the development of severe weather can be.

We were looking for pictures of thunderstorms and had been working on the project for a few spring days. One day it looked favorable for squall line development, and based on the best guess it would be wise to head northwest from Little Rock, putting relatively stable air behind, and photographing the squall line as it developed ahead of a cold front. Then there would be plenty of time to retreat back to Little Rock and tuck the airplane safely in its T-hangar before the rough stuff arrived.

Nothing was going on to the northwest and after milling around 50 to 75 miles out, talking to controllers, it was decided that there would be no photos today.

Heading back to base, the weather was typical of that in Arkansas when there is a strong southerly flow ahead of an advancing front or low. The cloud bases were between 2,000 and 2,500 feet above the ground and the cumulus clouds looked heavy and relatively fast-moving. The low-level turbulence was pretty heavy and the altimeter setting was low. When 30 miles or so

188   northwest of Little Rock, some clouds ahead had a very definite "don't fly beneath me" message. Dark bottoms and mighty churning were evident. Rain was beginning to fall from some of them, and even though they didn't yet classify as thunderstorms, their picture was taken based on meanness of appearance. It was possible to get around south of them, back to base.

Work done, I headed toward the lake for a sail. There was rain along the way with incredibly large drops that splattered the car mightily, a sign of extremely unstable air. Later on the radio I heard that about an hour after that cloud's picture had been taken, a town up to the northeast was blitzed by a tornado. Close examination of the pictures showed something that had every appearance of a funnel forming. Maybe that was it, maybe not. For every real tornado in the alley there are cloud formations that look enough like them to cause numerous reports of tornadoes by the public.

Another spring day, on a trip to Wichita, flying VFR in my Cherokee Six, I flew through a spell of strangely turbulent air. It was more disturbed than turbulent and the clouds above, based at perhaps 8,000 to 10,000 feet, had an odd churn to them and you could almost see the vertical development above those altitudes. It was the next day that a record tornado outbreak did incredible damage in Ohio.

Those are just a couple of examples of fascinating weather being as much a part of any route as the landmarks. There were beautiful trips over that route but in most there was some interesting weather with which to deal. And it is safe to say that I learned more about weather on that route than any other.

Florida   **189**

Of the routes to Florida from the northeast, a favorite one is over Norfolk, Virginia. If the weather is good, Norfolk is interesting to overfly because of the Navy presence there. Often large ships can be seen coming or going, occasionally there is a nuclear submarine leaving its unusual wake, and it's interesting to see if there are aircraft carriers in port. They sure look small from aloft. Later in the trip, the same interest is spurred at Jacksonville, home port for one or more carriers. But like most routes which are flown multiple times, the interest centers as much on the weather as the scenery. And for pilots flying to Florida in the winter to escape the cold, there are some rather harsh weather truths.

If you have a tailwind going, the weather in Florida is likely to be cooler than normal. The same wind that blows you there cools you while there. Also, if the weather is cold north and warm south, that means there is a front and during the time of year that most people want to go to Florida, this front is likely rather wide and quite wet. Dubbed the "Confederate Front" by some, it has interrupted countless VFR trips to Florida over the years. I remember one trip stopping at Wilmington for gas on the way to Florida and chatting with some pilots who were trying to get there VFR. We stopped for gas in Wilmington on the way back and they were still there.

Perhaps the most dramatic event on this route, though, is the formation of a nor'easter off the coast of North Carolina. These are the classic storms that dump large amounts of rain on the northeastern U.S., or, in the colder season, result in fancy blizzards. This is not an easy storm for the forecasters to predict because they develop and move out rather quickly and the timing and

190   the track the storm takes determines whether it turns into rain or snow. And while you might think that one of these storms would give you a quick trip to Florida, that is not always true. Even though the surface wind, and the low-level wind, might be from an easterly direction, it is a strong southwesterly flow aloft that supports the development of such a storm and guides it up the coast. When one of these is first developing, the low-level winds can be ferocious, too. I calculated a ground-speed of under 50 knots in my Cardinal RG one day while discovering that a low was indeed forming.

Between Joisey & Wichita

The most interesting part of flying west from New Jersey is that part of the trip that is over the Appalachian Mountains. They do different things in different seasons with one thing certain: If the weather is active, it is more active over these mountains. If there is ice out there, it is more prevalent over these mountains. If the wind is blowing, it is bumpy over these mountains. When I first started flying out of New Jersey, they loomed as insurmountable obstacles at times, and more than one trip to Wichita was made the long way, all the way around south of the mountains.

Over the Appalachians, whether along this route or to the south, is where many lessons about ice are learned. There is lifting, there is moisture, and there is cold. I have heard that when the airlines were flying DC-3s from Pittsburgh to New York, they would, after leaving Pittsburgh, climb westbound for a while to get some altitude before turning eastbound over the mountains. Altitude can be a great friend, too, but there have to be more favorable factors than just altitude to avoid ice over the mountains. I have found, though, that with

a turbocharged airplane they are usually manageable   **191**
as long as you are starting and finishing a reasonable
distance either side of the mountains, as opposed to
having to start or finish on the ground within the area,
and do all climbing or descending in the midst of the
icebox as opposed to on either side. That isn't to say
that there is no ice on either side—it can be debilitating
in either case.

ADVANTAGE

One of the great advantages of general aviation flying
is the diversity of airports you use and routes that you
fly. Maybe a few airports have special meaning for you,
as they do for me, and maybe some routes are flown so
often that they seem as familiar as the way to school
was in the third grade.

It's the other ones, the trips that are flown infre-
quently, that complete the picture. Coast-to-coast in a
day, with sunrise over the Grand Canyon. Los Angeles
northward over the Sierra Nevada to Boise; then over
the Salmon River area on up to Kalispell, Montana. Into
and out of the Bob Marshall Wilderness Area in Montana. Philadelphia to Bermuda in an Aztec. A lot of
flights go into the makeup of a flying career, whether
done as a profession or for personal or business transportation. Yours might be simpler, or far more complex,
but that doesn't make them any less, or more, meaningful.

9

Pilots—and the Rest
of the World

A S PILOTS we tend to live in our own world. There might indeed be 250,000,000 people down there in the United States, or many billions in the world, but they are all relegated to one level except where there are multistoried buildings. Look what we have: In the U.S. the two- or three-tenths of one percent of us who fly have all the air over this big country, at all altitudes; over the sea and in other countries the air is divided up among an even smaller percentage of the population. There is no question that there is a continuing competition for airspace in the U.S. as the airlines, the military, and general aviation stake their claims for exclusive use of airspace, preferential treatment in some airspace, or special favors. But there is a lot out there to go around.

The airspace closely relates to runway space in many areas. In fact, runway availability is the driving force in most places. Look at it this way: Even when the weather is bad, an airplane lands or takes off at Washington National Airport every minute. One passes an established point—the middle of the runway at field elevation—every 60 seconds. That is crowded.

The farther you fly away from the airport, the less crowded it gets because the airplanes are climbing to different altitudes and flying different tracks. The sky would only be half as crowded as the runway if every airplane came from the same place and flew at the same altitude, and flew away to the same place at the same altitude. Of course they don't do that, they go to different places at different altitudes and the farther you fly away from airports the less crowded the sky becomes. Perhaps the ultimate example of this is found when leaving the Oshkosh Air Show, where airplanes are launched every few seconds. As you fly away from the airport, it becomes harder and harder to spot other airplanes because they are progressively farther away, fanning out to almost as many destinations as there are departing airplanes.

BIG SKY, FEW PEOPLE

It is a big sky, but those of us who do fly have to come to grips with the fact that the public is obsessed with aviation, safety, crashes, and collisions. There are times when it is tempting to think this is all media hype, but it really isn't. It isn't possible to accurately say how many people are touched by aviation every day, but when you consider the people who ride airliners or fly their own, who have checks flown at night by the courier services, who ship or receive things using the overnight services, or who send or receive letters that go by air, it is a substantial percentage of the population. And

194   when 12,000 or so air traffic controllers went on strike
in the early '80s and the system was threatened, the
public realized that a majority of the population could
be affected by a relative handful of people in this business called aviation.

NEAR MISS OR NEAR HIT?

All the publicity about near collisions brought public
interest to a new high. A lot of the increase in near
collisions came from reporting procedures but a lot of
them were honest close calls. And there were some real
collisions to prove that if you get them close enough
together often enough, two will eventually collide. The
general public doesn't like this. In fact, they won't stand
for it. Pressure builds on Congress and soon legislation
is introduced to impose all sorts of airspace restrictions.
Aviation is in trouble. Or is it?

    If the public is convinced that the system is im-
proved to a point where the risk of collision is greatly
lessened, might they look more kindly at general aviation? Might the activity become better accepted if it is
not perceived to be a threat to the airline passenger?
Nobody knows the answers to these questions but one
thing is certain: Aviation—and this includes all pilots
and related industries—is going to have to address the
concerns of the public or be legislated out of business.

RESPONSIBILITY

Some years ago I was flying along, IFR in clouds, when
the controller called and said that I had traffic at 12
o'clock, opposite direction, that would probably be descending through my altitude. My first thought was one
of wonderment. How could that happen? A controller is

not supposed to do that. Then he added that the traffic was a military fighter, out of which the pilot had just ejected. I got a vector away, though I am sure the fighter could have caught me had it turned just right. I later learned that it did damage to little other than grass and dirt (and itself) on impact. I also learned something that disturbed me. The pilot had ejected from the fighter because the landing gear wouldn't extend. I wondered if that was an adequate excuse to turn loose thousands of pounds of hot metal and fuel to seek random targets in the air and on the ground.

The individual pilot could not be faulted. He followed standard operating procedures. But it was a reflection of a peculiar twist in how aviation sometimes addresses its responsibility to the public. Pull the handles, get out, transfer the risk to innocents. In the interest of minimizing the threat to a pilot, or perhaps in the interest of preserving the rights of a pilot, we have always seemed ready to perhaps endanger the lives and property of other people.

Before you hiss and boo over that, think about it.

HANGAR TALK

Perhaps the thing that we do as pilots that hurts most is tell tall tales. It is part of the lore of flying to build mild scrapes into death-defying acts. Many a time we stand around the airport and tell the stories without realizing that if a layman were listening, he would think us a reckless bunch of fools. More thought should be put into this. Flying is, and always has been, a very serious matter. If I listed the people that I have known as friends that have been lost in airplanes it would be a long list. None did themselves in on purpose. Rather, they failed to pay the proper attention to flying at a

196   critical moment. To make light of it by telling tall tales serves no real useful purpose. Rather, we should try to understand and cater to the feelings of nonpilots.

I thought of this one morning at breakfast, as four of us chatted. Actually, I listened because I didn't want to join in. Two of the other people were pilots. One was not a pilot, a person who later in the day would be riding home in a light airplane with one of the conversationalists. Only I would have ridden a bus after listening to the tales about mechanical malfunctions and scary times in light airplanes. These folks were certainly not conscious of what they were doing. It was just the time-honored business of pilots telling war stories. But it is something that we all have to overcome if we are to avoid extinction.

Whether or not they fly in light airplanes with us, the general public feels a relationship with us because they see our airplanes around airports when they fly on airliners. And there are only two ways for them to feel about our little airplanes. Either they see them as a threat to their security when riding on an airliner, or they see them as a nice way to get around—something they might consider if they ever have the need to travel enough to require an airplane of their very own.

It has been interesting to take people who express some animosity toward small airplanes on a trip. One friend of mine, whose company operates some classy jets, expressed discomfort over riding in another company's small jet yet rides comfortably in my Cessna 210. It is apparently perceived more as a personal automobile rather than a bit of expensive heavy iron. Another friend expressed wonderment as New York approach control gave us a scenic tour of the city, through the terminal control area, at a time when traffic was light.

People who don't fly today are the key to tomorrow, too. If aviation is to continue, it's the folks who are not now flying that will lead the way. Because of the age of people now flying, in 20 years very few of us will be active. In fact, British Airways didn't have a pilot under 35 in early 1987; because their mandatory retirement age is 55 that means that in 20 years not one pilot flying today will be still flying for the airline. They, like all other facets in aviation, have to maintain the feed of pilots to stay in business.

How do we, as pilots, do our part to interest people in the activity that we love, so that it will be around for future generations?

Perhaps the main thing is to package the usefulness and enjoyment of flying and steer clear of telling hairy tales. In doing radio and TV talk shows, I have been asked about scary times in flying. My answer is always that those are things that we work to avoid and that I really haven't had any. The day of the daredevil needs to be passed along to history, to be replaced by people who fly airplanes as if they were filled with eggs.

My grandmother flew with me on several trips and perhaps she was a good example of how some segments of the public feel about airplanes. At the age of 80, she rode in a new Bonanza from Fordyce, Arkansas, back to New Jersey once. In the vicinity of Charleston, West Virginia, we flew through a little bit of convective activity. Nothing really rough, but it was enough for her to talk for a long time about the storm that I flew her through. And in retrospect, I think that if I had explained it all to her in advance, she probably would have thought nothing of it. But for some reason I had been flying VFR and I had to call and get a clearance.

198   I was too busy to explain what was going on, and to her it probably appeared that I was about to be overwhelmed by events because of the busywork.

GOOD NEIGHBORS

Folks on the ground often perceive airplanes as a threat. It is true that the incidence of airplanes harming people on the ground is small, but when it does happen, it makes news. A collision between a business jet and a Piper Archer near Teterboro resulted in the jet plunging through an apartment house, killing one on the ground. The image is one of a person minding his own business, perhaps having a beer and some pizza while watching the evening news on TV, suddenly wiped out by an airplane.

On the other hand, airplanes can be projected as good. Some years ago I flew then-Governor Dale Bumpers of Arkansas around the state as he ran (very successfully) for the United States Senate. We used a Baron, either one donated by a supporter or one rented by his campaign committee, and it involved some late evenings and visits to more remote spots in the state. One fascinating thing to me was how people seemed to respect, almost revere, the machine that brought this charismatic candidate to them. It was good with a capital *G*.

Another item of interest was what the airplane did to expand Bumpers' ability to be anywhere at any time. He used the airplane very naturally, as an extension of his car or office or home. He would chat, or work thoughtfully on his speech as we rode along. He even concocted a speech that made fun of his pilot. That came one night as he addressed a graduating class at the Mena, Arkansas, high school. It was all in fun and

it wasn't an easy speech for him. He had told me earlier $\qquad$ **199**
that it was an unwritten rule that regardless of the heat
of a race, there could be no campaigning in commence-
ment speeches. There is a good lesson here for us. If we,
as pilots, can learn to avoid scary subjects when we are
speaking in public, or to nonpilots, perhaps a new day
in our relationship with the public will be allowed to
dawn in aviation.

10

The Future

VIATION has survived a lot of events that were at the time perceived to threaten its very existence. In 1973, when the Arabs imposed an oil embargo, our fuel supply was almost cut off. Not many years later the refinery that made the majority of the aviation gasoline burned. Another shortage. Product liability has been offered as a doomsday threat. At one point a leading aviation executive told me that the business was finished unless interest rates and inflation subsided. Both did, and aviation went into the biggest slump ever. As this is written the FAA is proposing sweeping new requirements for operation in much of the nation's airspace. But despite the perceived threats, and a public obsession with the dangers of flying, aviation will survive. The future is actually very bright, though it does offer a lot of challenges.

A young reader of our magazine wrote and said how much he enjoyed flying, but expressed the thought that in the future it might become so automated that the

202   The day will probably come when passengers will board a jetliner crewed by a 23-year-old pilot with 1,501 hours and an 18-year-old pilot with 251 hours, which would be perfectly legal. For this to work, and it will work, those pilots will have to have been trained differently from the way pilots are trained now. They will have to operate the airplane in a procedural manner—one that is laced more with what has been taught than what has been seen. The good old days when every airline captain had the benefit of years riding the right seat with curmudgeon perfectionists is gone. In the future it's going to be a short apprenticeship and then command. And when the pilot accepts that command, it's going to be by the book. The airlines of the future are going to have to be run more like the military than like a civilian business.

        This is good, too, not bad. The days when we can approach flying with a hell-for-leather outlook are gone. It just doesn't work that way any more. Airplanes have become precise machines that have to be operated in a precise manner. Anyone who doesn't care enough to do it properly just won't be able to play in the future. Some would argue that this turns it into an elitist activity. Maybe it does, to some extent, but that is tempered by a lot of things.

        For one, airline pilots of the future are going to make less money relative to other professions than they have in the past. For another, the use of personal and business airplanes is likely to evolve into a much more common activity. Gone will be the royal barge; the compact, efficient business airplane will be the choice—for most companies. There will surely still be the big-business jet for the heavy-duty movers and shakers of the world, but the more common of us will move about with less ado.

pilot would hardly be in the loop. Instead of being a pilot, the person in the pointy end of the airplane would become a computer operator, and the airplane would fly itself electronically. In fact, that already happens. I have flown a zero-zero landing in a Boeing 757 simulator in which the autopilot lands and stops the airplane. There is no way a human pilot could do that on a time-after-time, predictable basis, but the electronic pilot can do it. The important thing to realize, though, is that the human pilot has to be there, and has to be able to fly. As previously mentioned, automated airplanes have had to be landed under trying circumstances by real pilots.

In some of the newest fighters with fly-by-wire systems (meaning the airplane is flown through a computer, with electronic signals moving the controls) there have been accidents because the airplane and the computerized system can produce and withstand higher G loads than the human can. And when the human goes out of the loop a disaster follows. Even with the most sophisticated systems, the pilot can fly the airplane when he wishes. And there are times and places where even a routine arrival dictates that the pilot fly. A good example is that Canarsie approach to John F. Kennedy International Airport. It is a circling approach, flown using lead-in lights, and the only computer-piloting system built that can fly a Canarsie approach is a human, using what he sees and feels to maneuver the airplane around for a landing on Runway 13 Right or Left at JFK.

THE LINK

But something will change in the most important part of the link, the pilot. Because of the way events unfolded, there is and will be a shortage of experienced pilots.

pilot would hardly be in the loop. Instead of being a
pilot, the person in the pointy end of the airplane would
become a computer operator, and the airplane would fly
itself electronically. In fact, that already happens. I
have flown a zero-zero landing in a Boeing 757 simulator in which the autopilot lands and stops the airplane.
There is no way a human pilot could do that on a time-
after-time, predictable basis, but the electronic pilot can
do it. The important thing to realize, though, is that the
human pilot has to be there, and has to be able to fly.
As previously mentioned, automated airplanes have
had to be landed under trying circumstances by real
pilots.

In some of the newest fighters with fly-by-wire systems (meaning the airplane is flown through a computer, with electronic signals moving the controls) there
have been accidents because the airplane and the computerized system can produce and withstand higher G
loads than the human can. And when the human goes
out of the loop a disaster follows. Even with the most
sophisticated systems, the pilot can fly the airplane
when he wishes. And there are times and places where
even a routine arrival dictates that the pilot fly. A good
example is that Canarsie approach to John F. Kennedy
International Airport. It is a circling approach, flown
using lead-in lights, and the only computer-piloting system built that can fly a Canarsie approach is a human,
using what he sees and feels to maneuver the airplane
around for a landing on Runway 13 Right or Left at JFK.

THE LINK

But something will change in the most important part of
the link, the pilot. Because of the way events unfolded,
there is and will be a shortage of experienced pilots.

202   The day will probably come when passengers will board a jetliner crewed by a 23-year-old pilot with 1,501 hours and an 18-year-old pilot with 251 hours, which would be perfectly legal. For this to work, and it will work, those pilots will have to have been trained differently from the way pilots are trained now. They will have to operate the airplane in a procedural manner—one that is laced more with what has been taught than what has been seen. The good old days when every airline captain had the benefit of years riding the right seat with curmudgeon perfectionists is gone. In the future it's going to be a short apprenticeship and then command. And when the pilot accepts that command, it's going to be by the book. The airlines of the future are going to have to be run more like the military than like a civilian business.

This is good, too, not bad. The days when we can approach flying with a hell-for-leather outlook are gone. It just doesn't work that way any more. Airplanes have become precise machines that have to be operated in a precise manner. Anyone who doesn't care enough to do it properly just won't be able to play in the future. Some would argue that this turns it into an elitist activity. Maybe it does, to some extent, but that is tempered by a lot of things.

For one, airline pilots of the future are going to make less money relative to other professions than they have in the past. For another, the use of personal and business airplanes is likely to evolve into a much more common activity. Gone will be the royal barge; the compact, efficient business airplane will be the choice—for most companies. There will surely still be the big-business jet for the heavy-duty movers and shakers of the world, but the more common of us will move about with less ado.

The use of smaller airplanes for personal and busi-   203
ness transportation will see a resurgence. Only this
time the pilots will be better trained so they will be able
to use the airplanes at lower risk. The day will finally
come when we'll recognize that over half the population
does not have the natural coordination to safely operate
an airplane in other than perfect visual conditions.
Maybe that sounds restrictive to the extreme, but it's
not. It is simply true. Aviation is, and always has been,
a province of the quick and the dead. Just as some of us
don't have the mental ability to master trigonometry, or
the ear to master music, or the eye to paint like Rem-
brandt, some of us don't have the natural ability to fly
well. And the sooner that is acknowledged and built
into the system, the better.

It is sad but true that few of us who are "in" aviation today comprise what is a basis for the future. We
are here, and we do fly, but the new basis is only now
slowly coming on board. Why aren't the current folks
going to shape the future? Mainly because we are to
some extent jaded. A hundred grand for a Skyhawk!
The only reason that is shocking to us old guys is because we remember when they were fifteen grand. And
just as a New York area pilot will sit for three hours to
get across the George Washington Bridge on the way to
Teterboro and then bitch about a 15-minute delay for an
IFR clearance, most of us think that it's okay for inflation to rage in other areas but not in aviation. For us to
really take part in the future, we will have to change a
lot of our ways of thinking, and I doubt that a majority
are willing to do that. The new folks coming into aviation lack our handicaps.

There is no question that electronics have made the grandest strides in the past 20 years and will probably do the same in the next 20 years. Surely in the future we will have stability augmentation systems in light airplanes, systems that will make the airplane go straight except when the pilot makes it turn. This was actually included on all Mooneys for a while, under the name "positive control," or "PC," and it only makes sense that it become an integral part of every airplane. In most accidents involving a loss of control, roll control is lost first. This simply cries out for an electronic solution.

The pilot of the future is going to be willing to pay the bucks, and fit into the system, but he is unlikely to put up with some of the easily fixable foibles of airplanes that we have endured for years. The battle cry will be to make it good, not cheap. Few people will be willing to fly airplanes that are so basically unstable that they can be in an unrecoverable maneuver in less than a minute. And that isn't in conflict with the thought that future pilots will come from only those who have some natural talent. The challenge of flying is increasing, not decreasing, and the airplane as well as the pilot has to be upgraded to meet that challenge.

Will we have composite airplanes? I have a friend who thinks I am terrible because I am skeptical about the use of composites in airplanes. But I feel this way for good reason. In watching the composite airplanes that have been developed, they are always heavier than metal counterparts. The Beech Starship is far heavier than the Piaggio Avanti. The Glasair kit-built airplane is heavier than the metal Venture. The composite Learfan wound up with an empty weight that was actually greater than the airplane's initial design gross weight.

The Starship has no apparent price advantage over the Piaggio; in kits there is little price advantage although there the composite's advantage in building simplicity might well mean fewer hours of labor to build the airframe. But not a lot less in the case of a fully equipped IFR airplane, where only about 25 percent of the labor is devoted to the airframe. If anything, I have always felt that the false hope offered by composites played a big role in the slump in aircraft sales seen in the 1980s. A lot of people might well have felt that a big breakthrough was just around the corner and decided to fly on in the old airplane until the new lightweight plastic airplanes came on line.

Rather than composite airframes being used to cut cost and reduce weight, the big breakthrough in production airplanes might well be in systems. Most of the parts in airframes are devoted to the electrical, vacuum, and hydraulic systems and avionics systems. This is where the maintenance goes, too. Wires, hoses, and pipes are expensive to assemble and to fix. When I open the cowling on my P210 and look at the amount of monkey-motion under there for the purpose of moving electricity and air around, I am always amazed. There just has to be a simpler way. I was visiting King Radio's hangar one day, and there were several people at work building a wiring harness for the avionics in a Cessna Caravan. If all that wire were laid end to end, it would take the Caravan a lot more than a minute to fly from one end to the other. Whether the answer to this is in fiber optics, or something akin to a printed circuit board, I know not. But when it comes to weight and labor savings, there is probably more gold to be mined in systems than anywhere else.

POWERPLANTS

It is often said that there can be no new generation of airplanes until we get new powerplants. Not too many years ago the then-president of Beech, Frank Hedrick, said that all their airplanes would be powered by turbines in 10 years. Almost 20 years later the Bonanzas and Barons were still coming off the line with piston engines. What didn't happen was the development of a turbine engine that was competitive in price with a piston engine of the same horsepower.

There is a bit of a myth surrounding turbines that might be likened to the composite myth. That myth relates to power. The simple fact is that if a turbine and a piston put out the same amount of power, the airplane will climb and cruise at the same speed. And the turbine will burn more fuel. The turbine's hourly operating cost might be comparable even though it burns more fuel, because its time between overhauls is greater and routine maintenance should be less. Fuel is a bit less costly, too. But, unfortunately, there is not likely to be a price breakthrough, and the turbine will probably continue to command a premium price in return for its greater reliability and lower vibration level. The turbine also has the advantage of producing more horsepower from less engine weight, which makes possible such new designs as the Aerospatiale/Mooney-developed TBM 700, a 300-knot single. All this is good, but the inexpensive turbine is still over the horizon.

Porsche

One good and interesting development in 1987 was the certification of the Porsche aircraft engine. A derivation of the engine used in the 911 automobile, the compact

six-cylinder opposed engine is in the low- to high-200-   **207**
horsepower range, depending on the fuel used (autogas
for the lowest horsepower, avgas for the higher horsepower and turbocharged engines) and the amount of
boost taken from the turbocharger on the two most
powerful engines. The highest rating now seen for the
engine is 280; at that it could power singles up through
the Bonanzas and 210s, or light twins like the Baron.

The specific fuel consumption (pounds per hour to
create horsepower) is lower for the Porsche engine than
for other pistons, and there is an additional kicker. Because it has automatic mixture control, the mixture is
always properly leaned. This will ensure additional fuel
savings because few of us do a perfect job of leaning the
mixture at all times.

The Porsche engine will cost more than a Lycoming
or a Continental, and at first sight this makes folks
skeptical about the chances for success. But flying it is
a revelation. It is operated with a single-lever power
control—prop and mixture are automatic—and the engine is cooled by a large fan so there's no worry about
either hot running or sudden cooling. It takes care of
itself. And it is as quiet and smooth as the best turboprop. Managing the noise that the air makes as it flows
over the airframe becomes the biggest challenge, once
the Porsche engine is installed. And with automatic
mixture and electronic ignition, it has what cars have
had for years but we've heretofore been unable to have
in airplanes. The success of this engine will be quite
important to the next generation of airplanes, and its
price should be compared to that of a turboprop, not a
piston.

A collision-avoidance system is inevitable for airline aircraft, whether it is useful or not, and they will also all have wind shear detection equipment. Transponders will eventually switch from Mode C to Mode S, enabling data links and perhaps some elimination of voice communications with air traffic controllers. Navigation might eventually evolve into a satellite-based system though the pages in this book will probably turn yellow before you see the absolute end of the current Vortac-based navigational system, especially for those flying in the lower altitudes.

The important thing about the future is that we do have one finite resource that limits traffic and that cannot be enhanced much with electronics. Airport and runway capacity is the drive behind setting limits on how much traffic can be handled in an area. There is no way to foresee anything that will, for example, allow a lot more airplanes to be handled in the major areas than are now handled.

While the limiting factor is runway time for airliners at the major terminals, general aviation faces not only the air traffic problem, but also a space problem on the ground. For example, at Teterboro airport in New Jersey, the closest full-capability general aviation airport to New York, there are IFR delays at busy times but the airport remains generally accessible and the delays there are probably far less than for a person trying to get through the Lincoln Tunnel into Manhattan in a car. But the ability of Teterboro to absorb more based aircraft is limited by ramp and hangar space. And if anything is going to change the face of airports in the future, this will.

Look for airports to eliminate runways running in

all directions to make available more space on the   **209**
ground. This is already done in California, where
smaller airports have the capacity to serve more based
aircraft than some rather large airports in the northeast,
the other crowded area. Another thing that will probably happen is that people will drive farther to fly than
they do now. From my house in central New Jersey, the
closest airline airport is an hour's drive away. The closest good place to sail my boat is an hour's drive away.
Yet I want my airplane to be fifteen minutes away. That
is ideal, and I hope it stays that way. But we can't
expect the airplane to be immune forever to the things
that affect other activities.

SHAPE OF THE FLEET

One class of airplanes almost passed into history in the
'80s. Where the light and medium piston twins were the
darlings of the '60s and '70s, they sold by the handful in
the '80s and the values of used twins plummeted. At
some auctions, five-year-old twins brought hardly ten
percent of what they would cost new if built today. A
number of factors contributed to this slump, and these
factors will continue to affect what we fly in the future.

Insurance is a big item. If a person does not have
a lot of experience in twins, insurance might range from
prohibitively expensive to unavailable. This isn't due to
petulance on the part of insurors, it is due to their experience with light twins. Even if a pilot has twin experience, it's a sure bet that the insuror will require that he
attend school on the specific type when he buys a new
airplane. One pilot with many years' experience in Barons bought a Pressurized Baron and was required to go
to school before being insurable. This seemed excessive
to the pilot, but the P-Baron is indeed enough different

210   from the others to require training. It operates in a different environment and requires more powerplant management. The best place to learn that is in school.

    The direct operating cost of a twin is a driving factor, too. I was flying along in my P210 discussing this with another pilot. We had just heard of an excellent Pressurized Aerostar selling for a price lower than my P210 would bring, and I wondered aloud if those of us with enough twin time to be insurable were missing a bet by not buying one of the airplanes at a bargain price. Then I thought about the doubling of maintenance costs, since most maintenance is on engines. Two engines and props to overhaul. Double the gas at a speed only 20-percent faster. More noise and vibration. It didn't take me long to dispel any notion of switching.

    Maybe the fact that the average pilot flying light twins failed to find the safety that he thought he bought in the airplane was what led to the demise of the light twin. That shouldn't have been. But if this type airplane is to be part of the personal/business fleet of the future, we are going to have to look at it in a different way. The training requirement is going to have to be much greater, with recurrent training required. With that, the airplanes might achieve their safety potential. Then perhaps they will become popular once again.

TURBOPROP SINGLES

A joint venture between Mooney and the general aviation division of Aerospatiale on the TBM 700 offers the promise of the first single-engine turboprop personal/business airplane. This airplane should appeal to the kind of people who used to be attracted to medium twins, as the acquisition cost (about a million bucks) is about the same. The advantages the TBM 700 will offer

are lower operating cost and better performance. The   211
airplane will be a 300-knot cruiser, which is 60 or 70
knots faster than the better twins. While there won't be
much if any saving on fuel, engine maintenance will be
substantially less. If there is one specific class that will
proliferate as factory-built, it is the turbine single. It is
not all romance, either. Cessna's big Caravan is a real
worker. In most other areas there will be fewer different
models than in the past but we can hope that the airplanes that are built will be ever more reliable and
efficient and will perform well.

BIG BROTHER

Unfortunately, in determining the future of aviation the
government plays a bigger role than any other single
entity. This is too bad because the government has no
vested interest in making aviation more attractive to
more people. It is true because aviation is, and has
always been, a national activity. It is, by necessity,
regulated by the feds. Over the years a reasonable job
has been done, even-handed in relation to general aviation and the airlines. But one thing that changed with
airline deregulation—the profile of the "average" airline traveler—brought a new dimension to the politics
of aviation.

More of the general public is more interested in
aviation than ever in history, and all aviation has to
make peace with this. The public-relations effort has to
change to one of accommodation between user groups
rather than confrontation. There can simply be no acri-
monious public debates between the various interests
in aviation. If aviation doesn't show that it can solve its
own problems, then the public, through the Congress,
will settle the matter. And if you think FAA solutions

212 are uncomfortable, anything that comes from Congress will be far worse.

STANDARDS OF THE FUTURE

With that background, it is clear that the direction of aviation will be set by the FAA. The best hope is that it will be done with at least some input from user groups.

The FAA sets rules and enforces standards in building and flying airplanes. The standards that are set for building airplanes have often been held up as increasing the cost of certifying airplanes but, really, they do not specify anything that a conscientious builder would not do. And in some areas the FAA has allowed things to pass that are questionable. An example is in the systems that power flight instruments. While the FAA folks who dictate pilot standards were letting the need for partial panel flying fade into the background, the FAA airplane folks were allowing airplanes certified for IFR flight to be built with single and not overly-reliable instrument power systems. In the future, that will change. The FAA might finally start looking at what has been causing trouble and require that airplanes offer a pilot more options in case of trouble.

It has long been held that people flying airplanes for hire are held to a higher standard than people who operate airplanes for personal or business reasons. The result of that has been that many not-for-hire people do not operate to the highest possible standard. That, too, will change. Through a combination of FAA and insurance company requirements, we are likely to evolve into everyone operating at and being held to the highest possible standard. The public is going to demand it.

There was an airplane accident clip on TV the

morning this was written. What appeared to have been   213
a single-engine retractable had crashed through the
wall of an apartment house in California. Just in the
past year or so, a twin went through a rooftop in New
York, another twin took out some row houses, yet another twin went through the roof of a mall and into a
line of children waiting to see Santa Claus, and a military jet took out a motel. Whenever these things happen, they make the national news. We might contend
that the pilots involved are not representative, but they
are. Just as the airline crew that makes the news for
days by crashing a jetliner is thought of as a generic
airline crew, the general aviation pilot who crashes into
a house is a generic general aviation pilot, whether we
like it or not, or agree with the assessment. And if the
public is not convinced that the people flying those airplanes are doing their 100-percent best to avoid such
things, they will demand (and get) changes. Thus the
evolution to the highest possible standard for all flight
operations.

NOT ALL BAD

This evolution won't necessarily harm the activity. In
fact, in the long run it could help the activity very much.
If flying becomes more professional and more socially
acceptable, it will attract a new customer base. Gone
will be the folks who revel in telling scary war stories,
to be replaced by pilots whose pride comes not from
defying gravity and escaping death, but from flying a
routine flight of which they are proud.

In a recent seminar, one questioner took me to task
for never talking in my magazine column about any
mistakes that I make when flying. Well, when I do err,
I confess. I wrote a while back about busting an alti-

214 tude. But I do try very hard not to make mistakes. Flying is not some experimental venture, where you bumble along making mistakes and covering them with bursts of brilliance. It's a deadly serious business that demands 100-percent attention. The accident rate in the past has not reflected that a majority of the pilots realize this. It will be different in the future, or there won't be much flying allowed.

AIRSPACE AND AIRPORTS

Whatever happens in the certification of airplanes and fliers will be overshadowed as the FAA changes the nature and structure of the air in which we fly. Not only must they work to minimize the risk of midair collisions, they must also do everything possible to increase the capacity of the airport-airways system. The good news is that this is possible, though we might in the future have to go farther to reach our airplanes if we are major metropolitan-area fliers.

THE PEOPLE

Despite all the things that will change, one thing will remain the same in aviation. The people who are attracted to the activity are, on balance, the nicest bunch of people you will ever meet. When I think of my young friends in aviation and my old friends in aviation, they are all a lot alike. From my father, 85 at this writing, to the college students that we fly with at the National Intercollegiate Flying Association airmeet, all have a common bond. And in the time that I have been in this business it has never changed. It is a hard thing to quantify, but flying does, I think, broaden a person's outlook. The independent responsibility helps build

character, and people who fly tend to have a greater   215
interest in everything that is going on than people who
do not fly. Maybe this is because relatively few of us
can do what most of the people on earth can't do. From
the Auburn University War Eagle Flying Team to the
old-timers who flew airplanes with OX-5 engines, pilots
are a fine lot. I have met thousands of people who fly
and can count off the ones who weren't enjoyable to be
with on my fingers.

BEST NEWS OF ALL

The nature of pilots is just one bit of good news. Equally
important is the fact that the basic freedom to use airplanes in the same manner that we use automobiles is
likely to remain in the United States for a long time to
come. The restrictions that are placed on the use will
allow this freedom to be tolerated by the general public.
Hopefully, the unfortunate word *tolerated* can be replaced by something more pleasant in the future. That,
my flying friend, is up to us, you and me. We, all of
us—airline, military, and general aviation, along with
feds involved in aviation—have, by our actions, planted
some seeds of distrust. And only by working very hard
to make every flight the perfect flight can we recover
and fly on to bigger and better things.

Index

217